a 95

OAKTON COMMUNITY COLLEGE

Des Plaines. Illinois

Saturday Parent

SATURDAY PARENT

A Book for Separated Families

by Peter Rowlands

CONTINUUM : New York

1980
The Continuum Publishing Corporation
815 Second Avenue, New York, N.Y. 10017

Printed in the United States of America

Library of Congress Cataloging in Publication Data
Rowlands, Peter.   Saturday parent.
   Bibliography.
     1. Parenting, Part-time—United States.
I. Title.
HQ755.8.R68   306.8'7   80-36801
ISBN 0-8264-0026-4

Contents

Preface

Plenty of volumes provide encouragement and guidance for parents who for one reason or another are bringing up a family by themselves. This is a book for the *other* parent—the one who only sees the children on Saturdays, or once every two weeks, or for the occasional week during the year. Nowadays both men and women are becoming Saturday parents in large numbers. I have tried to arrange my material so that it can be helpful both to fathers and to mothers. Case histories have been collected and analyzed with this in mind.

Many of those I have talked to were convinced their situation was unique, which often made them pessimistic or depressed. Of course there is something that is individual about every family. But the way they spoke of their problems suggested a conviction that they were rare, isolated cases. This is linked with an apologetic attitude about the role they play, and a lack of communication with other Saturday parents. Being apologetic is pointless, because it helps nobody. And communication may as well start with this book.

By no means all I spoke to were pessimistic: some had a great deal of success to report, and put me in touch with some very impressive and well-balanced children and young adults. I want to pass on some of the things that they learnt.

I have been fortunate in meeting a lot of people who have been happy to talk to me, and who have been very generous with their time and with the details of their family life. If you are reading this now, and you contributed to my understanding, please accept my sincere thanks. Significantly, many of you asked for advice. I only wish I could have helped you more.

Sometimes I spoke to parents who had custody of their children. Their perception of how relationships could fare between their children and the absent parents was often very valuable. My thanks to them. I must also thank another group, whose advice was often refreshingly direct—the children of separated parents, of all ages.

Social workers, doctors, judges, teachers, and psychologists have also been particularly kind and anxious to put me on what they felt was the right track. Many have conflicting views, but whenever possible I have tried to draw on their accumulated experience and wisdom. I thank them very much.

Whenever case-history material appears, changes have been made to minimize the risk of individuals being recognized. If you suspect that a case is similar to yours but you feel that somehow I've got it wrong, remember that this is deliberate, to save embarrassment.

The original idea for the book came from Susi Hock-Lovell. Her suggestions, help and criticism have all been wonderful.

1: Does It Matter?

I f you have young children, but are not living with them, you probably want to take advantage of what the law calls "access." From time to time you make arrangements to see them. Whether you are already doing this or intend to do so, you very likely make use of that day of the week when you don't have to go to work but the stores, restaurants, and places of entertainment are still open. You are in fact a Saturday parent. This book is for you.

It does not matter if you find Sunday a more convenient day for visiting, or whether you meet frequently or rarely. Your children may be very young or almost adult. You may live near by or in another country. You are more likely to be a father than a mother, simply because more mothers are given custody of their children when there is a divorce. But, if you happen to be a mother and a Saturday parent, you are kept in mind throughout the book, and there is a chapter reserved mainly for you.

Perhaps you are a parent who has got custody, yet you are curious about the other side of the coin. You may simply take an active interest in children, as a social worker, teacher, clergyman, or anyone who sees a lot of children with difficult problems and tries to help them. You could also very possibly be a child whose parents live apart. Everyone is welcome aboard this book. But while I am writing it is primarily with the Saturday parents themselves in my mind. They are the real "you" to whom I'm talking.

A lot of Saturday parents I've met seem nervous or apologetic about their role. This applies more to the time when they are not yet used to their status, or when the separation or the divorce is still raging. (The point in time when a court makes a decision is of course irrelevant to this.) Many of the more nervous newcomers are surprised when they come to appreciate that far from being alone or unusual the Saturday parent is a widespread species whose numbers are growing.

The next time you find yourself near a snack bar at a zoo, or in a little restaurant by a swimming pool or a recreation ground, take a closer look at the family groups. There will be some children on their own. These may be well-behaved or antisocial, gloomy or cheerful. But typically they will be trying each other out, perhaps arguing about how to spend their money, whether to join up with other children or not, or whether it is time to go on and do something else. They are unconcerned about adults, but usually eager to impress each other. Sometimes they are eyed rather enviously by the children who are with their parents. Whether the parents are holding the reins loosely or firmly, the children are obviously aware of their presence, and they adapt their behavior accordingly. Usually they sense that they are having to obey rules, while some others are not. Depending on their age and personality, they may have a particularly strong attachment to one of the parents, and they may be trying to attract attention. Some of them will be noisy, others quiet. But they are all part of the "normal" scene as it is generally understood. Maybe that is why snack bars and restaurants exist at zoos and swimming pools.

But there is a third category too. Over in the corner, there is a man with two children, let's say a girl and a boy, aged ten and six respectively. The man is trying to make conversation with his daughter, who cannot find the right words for talking to him. His son is trying to get as much of the action as he can. Now and then he tugs at his father's hand and asks for another ice cream. Then he interrupts and asks a riddle, one that he's already aired, two weeks ago. He may walk behind his father's chair and offer to demonstrate a judo hold. This irritates his father: normally he might like it, but just now it is too much of a good thing. It is very distracting while he is trying to get his daughter to talk more about her life at school, her friends, her pet hamster—*anything*. She may get herself off the hook eventually, by asking, "And where are you living now, Daddy? You told me once, but I've forgotten. . . ."

This father is in fact a Saturday parent. My book is about him. It also applies—at an increasing rate nowadays—to some mothers who are Saturday parents. But they are mostly fathers. This is why I talk about "him," and "his children," except in Chapter 8, which is concerned specifically with the Saturday mother's particular problems.

Back to that snack bar. Can there be *other* Saturday parents with their Saturday children? Yes, there's another group, similar in composition, over on the other side. And, yes, there's another one too. In this case, the father has a tougher job. He is wheeling a stroller, while a five-year-old runs ahead of him. He is praying to God that there is enough room for them to sit down—preferably in a corner where they will not be too conspicuous. At least one of these groups will at some point be joined by a woman who is not the children's mother. With some practice you can distinguish that scene from the "straight" families too. It presents some differences and some problems of its own which will be explored in this book.

Why are there so many of these single-parent groups, all in the snack bar? When somebody starts becoming a Saturday parent, he tends to believe that he and his circumstances are individual. This is a natural feeling, since he has just gone through an emotional crisis and he probably feels very strongly about his relationship with his child or children. In fact, he is one of many. Their number is growing. In any average street, there will be one family in five where the father is temporarily or permanently living away from home. (In some cases he has been replaced—again on either a temporary or a permanent basis.) Only about half of these one-parent homes involve a formal divorce. The exact status of the relationship between the original parents in the other cases may vary from time to time, for example through reconciliation. If the trend continues, we can expect that there will be one family in four where one parent is missing. Note that the figures are linked to, but not the same as, the divorce rate (see Table 1). There are states in the USA where one-parent families are approaching two in five. Of course, not all absentee parents turn up on Saturday, and some never come around at all. But there are plenty who do, and they are the people who appreciate it when zoos and swimming pools, museums and so on remain open throughout the year.

Teachers' attitudes towards the results of this trend, as they see them in the classroom, vary from one school to another and particularly from one kind of district to another. The negative side (e.g. "He's behind the rest of his class and he's disturbed, but of course he comes from a broken home") recurs, especially when a parent's departure means less attention and less affection. But some see a positive side too. In a middle-class school in Toronto a teacher who deals mainly with Grade 9 (fourteen-year-old) boys and girls had this to say:

"There are thirty-three in my class, of whom nineteen come from split homes. To be frank with you, I have more trouble with the kids from two-parent families. I believe there are three reasons for this. First, each parent, when they're divorced, is giving more of their time to their children. Second, there are fewer disagreements on discipline, pulling the kids this way and that. And then fi-

TABLE 1
One-Parent Families: Estimates for English-Speaking Countries

	Divorce rate (1978)	Proportion of families where one parent is absent
Australia	1 in 4	1 in 6
Canada	2 in 7	1 in 4
New Zealand	1 in 5	1 in 7
South Africa	2 in 5	1 in 3
UK	1 in 4	1 in 5
USA	1 in 3	2 in 7

Divorce rate is higher than incidence of one-parent families after the following are taken into account:

Factors making divorce rate *higher*
More divorces involve childless couples; divorce rate is increasing more among young marrieds who tend to have shorter separation periods, quicker divorces (and fewer children); reconciliations post-divorce; some two-parent families have bypassed marriage.

Factors making divorce rate *lower*
Separation precedes divorce; separation happening without divorce; unmarried mothers who keep their children.

Sources: Census data; other government statistics; estimates from welfare bureaus.

nally there's less fighting going on around them, and they get pulled into arguments less often.''

This is *not* an argument for divorce. It simply says: Don't write the children off just because their parents have split up. You can help them transcend the situation.

Very often a parent who moves out starts living in a smaller place, whether his own apartment or a room in somebody else's house. Wherever it is, whether he is there from choice or economic necessity, the chances are that it has not much to offer an active child. Sometimes he may feel a little ashamed of it. Then again, he may be living with somebody else now, and he may prefer to avoid or limit his child's encounters with this person for the time being. There is of course the family home itself. More likely than not, he is not welcome there to do as he pleases. The surroundings that he knows, and where he is known, may make him feel uncomfortable. He is especially worried—although he may not admit this—that if the visit is organized in the neighborhood one of two agonizing things may happen. First it may rain, or his child may become bored, and ask with irresistible logic why they cannot go home now: ''Mommy won't mind!'' Second, if there is no sense of something special going to happen, his child may prefer to stay at home, play with his friends, help his mother, or just watch television. No parent likes the idea of being passed over. So he organizes some kind of event. Not being rich, and sometimes having to choose what will suit different age groups at the same time, he may opt for the park, the swimming pool, the museum . . . and the zoo, the cinema or the fairground when he has rather more spare cash.

It is in bad weather that the Saturday parent and his child are most in evidence. *Any* family can go for a walk along the lake front on a warm summer's day. But who are those breaking into a run as they round a corner and see a restaurant in mid-March, with scarves wound tight around their necks? Who else but the Saturday parent would choose such a bleak outing?

This is not meant to be like a bird book, however, showing how you can track the species down and follow them through binoculars. Saturday parents often want help and encouragement.

Let's get back to that snack bar, where there was a kind of triangle situation with nobody satisfied—the father, his ten-year-old daughter and his six-year-old son. The father remembers, suddenly, that his children were said to have gone to visit his former mother-in-law the previous weekend. "How's Granny?" he asks.

"Oh, she's fine," says his daughter Emma, without much thought.

"No, she's not!" shouts six-year-old Donald, abandoning his attempts at a judo hold. "She's got brok—brok—er, something in her throat. She was in bed."

Emma just sighs. "He means bronchitis."

"That can be rather serious at her age," their father says. "What did she look like to you, Emma,—or did you have to stay away?"

"No, we went in to see her, but we had to stay at the end of the bed," Emma reports. (Donald has tried to interrupt with his version of the events, but he is quietened with the words "This is Emma's turn. I'll ask *you* to tell me all about it in a minute.") "She looked very tired," Emma goes on.

"That's often what you feel like with bronchitis. It wears you out, trying to talk and breathe properly. Did she talk much, Donald? Did she seem happy?"

"Oh yes, I think so," says Donald. "She gave us some chocolate."

"Do you know something that would cheer her up? You two can choose some animal postcards for her at the zoo shop, and you can send them to her with your love. Just tell her to get well soon. She'll like that. Don't worry about stamps, I've got some. What are you going to send her, Donald?"

His son announces that he will buy the postcard of the biggest snake he can find, which makes Emma laugh and declare that her brother is disgusting. Their mood cheers up considerably when they *find something that they can do together*. This means more than just sitting down and watching television, or ordering a hamburger and a milkshake. If it is a shared activity, in which everybody contributes and nobody gets ignored, two things happen. First, people forget about the problems of not seeing each other so often, and they become less stilted. Second, they really do start to learn much more about one another than if they ask and answer direct questions. The questions and answers are often all formality with each participant trying hard to say the right thing. But discussing somebody else whom they all know, deciding that they can do something for her, and then going off to do it together—that is *real life*. The concern that Emma and Donald have for their grandmother, and the way they set about choosing good postcards to send (Donald's need to impress, for example, with a big snake), are all valuable information—if only their father is prepared to see it as such. It can tell him far more about his children than answers like "Oh yes, Daddy, things are all right at school now."

Shared activity of this kind doesn't allow time to stop and wonder what they should be doing or saying. It is also a far better guarantee that the children will be interested in coming out together with their Saturday parent on future occasions. If they know that they are more likely to get involved in something active, they don't worry about submitting to yet another awkward question-and-answer session. They realize also that they will be more than just co-spectators at some event.

It also brings an occasional unlooked-for bonus. Emma asks her father if he is going to send a card as well. He answers, "No, I don't think so," and then hesitates. He senses that she wants a reason for this. "Do you want to know why?"

Emma says that she thinks she knows, but Donald wants to know. "Don't you *like* Granny, Daddy?" he demands with his usual tact.

"Well, listen," their father explains quietly. "I *do* like her, and I'm sorry she's ill, but she was very sad about my moving away from your mummy, and I just think it would upset her if she got a postcard from me at the moment."

"It's quite true," Emma tells him. "Granny used to look at us, and just start crying. She never talks about you."

Her father smiles. "That can't be very cheerful, when someone takes a look at you and bursts into tears."

Donald gives an imitation wail, which he announces is "just like Granny." The others have to laugh, although Emma tells him he *is* being disgusting again.

"It's not good being sad all the time," their father adds.

"No, I'm not sad," Emma claims.

She knows this is not entirely so, and her father knows it too.

Each knows, for once, that the other knows. They exchange a closer smile than for many a week. The granny episode had served to draw Emma out, to bring a little bit of the darkness in her mind up to the surface. They had looked at it together and felt better for doing so. It did not expose everything—and the feelings were so strong that this was probably just as well. But it helped them to unwind a little, and to talk naturally about it. They all went to their separate homes happier that day, feeling that they had really done something.

Not every parent who has moved away from the family home actually wants to have the kind of experience that I have just described. There are several reasons. An obvious one is lack of interest in the children. But more commonly, to judge from talking to Saturday parents, they either feel they are going to be embarrassed, hurt, or made to feel guilty, or they have decided on a new life plan and do not want anything to get in its way.

I believe that both these reasons are misguided and eventually self-defeating. At the same time, it is easier to understand than to condemn anyone for feeling this way.

Being embarrassed and guilty is far more likely to happen when you meet with your children very infrequently, or if you haven't seen them for a long time. It is much less likely to be a problem if you find something that you and the children can enjoy doing together. This is why avoidance of the pain often leads a separated parent back into a bigger dose of pain. A similar point can be made about starting a fresh life with another partner. Nothing is ever begun totally from scratch. If you cannot live with certain memories, or cannot adapt to young people from the past who have a claim on you and need you, then the future is going to be under threat.

Do children *need* two parents anyway? This is a question that has to be answered. It is easy to say, "yes, of course, since they are biologically equipped with two parents from the start, and because that is the way society is meant to continue." This kind of answer will not do nowadays. Biological need ends soon enough. Society need not necessarily be right in all its demands, and is often proved wrong. Blind faith in social institutions, the classical family included, is not characteristic of our time. Nor should it be. The real answers to the question have to come from solid information, and from objective interpretation of that information.

The pointers that are relevant are evidence of the kind of roles in bringing up children that both parents play in the normal course of events, and how these roles help their children; and the evidence that exists about what happens to children whose parents break up, so that they are denied the benefit of some of these roles.

During the early years, children usually have a good chance of getting to know two adults really well. This can be the mother and the father. It is not always so, however, and it may be that where the parents are totally committed to the hard work ethic, so that both are away from their children five or six days a week, every week, with the club, fishing, or golf on Sundays, then a grandparent and a daycare center attendant may be the best known individuals in a child's life. But normally it will be the mother and father. Take one away, and early experience of what an adult is like, and of how a close relative behaves is reduced by fifty per cent. A child then becomes *undernourished,* from the point of view of learning about people. Mothers are often very busy people, and competition for their attention is often fierce. But they are usually around, a comforting presence in the foreground or the background, a source of food, of help, and of basic comfort. Fathers are often less harassed when they make their appearance in the evening. They are experiencing a change of pace after work (even when confronted by a temper tantrum) and they typically constitute a different character of experience when they get close to their child. They are also different people, doing different things, and they are under close observation.

A very intelligent six-year-old once asked me, "Do you work for IBM too?" I looked at him curiously, and said "No." Then I realized that his father and several of his father's close friends worked at that large company. For him, the outside world of men expanded outwards from his concept of "father." He was probably paying me a compliment, by endowing me with a characteristic that these male people who went out to work seemed to share. Gradually, he would learn that there are a great many variations in jobs, temperament, behavior, and interests that exist beyond his father and his IBM network. But he had the advantage of a standard, a man whom he was starting to understand, and whom he had long since started to love and admire.

The danger when talking about this important part of parental contact is to fall into line with conventional sex roles too early. In families where roles are reversed, where mother is the breadwinner and father is nearly always around, a child takes in different messages. These preconceptions of what men and women do are not necessarily "wrong," although they are still unusual. The child will realize later on that his parents were rather exceptional. But he will still have benefited from a wide range of perceptions about parent adults and how they relate to himself, a child, from the following points of view: how they treat him; how they do things together, both separately from him and with him; how they differ from each other, in interests, personality, humor—all the "fine tuning" that makes somebody an individual. By contrast, a child who sees only one parent sees just one side of the coin.

Of course there is a great deal that a parent can do to enrich that child's environment and to avoid making him too dependent emotionally on the one person. Nor do I dispute the enormous potential value of older brothers and sisters, of friends of the family, or of the "Big Brothers" movement. These help. But they are not equivalent to fathers.

Children who know that there was somebody around for a while whom they called "Daddy," and who left without returning, are missing something important. Sometimes they deny this, but the denial often lacks conviction. It means they are being as positive as they can about the situation, and their attitude commands respect. But there is a gap there which is very hard to fill.

Earlier, I talked about the positive side of a father's contribution. The negative side is what happens when the father withdraws. It used to be the case that fatherless children were taunted at school, to remind them of their loss, as if it made them inferior. Probably this still goes on to some extent. However, the major problems are the feelings that take place *within* the child as opposed to those which are stirred up from outside.

Children who can maintain close links with their father, even after he has split off from the family, get the benefit of being able to talk about him at school more easily, as well as being able to gain from his love, his experience, and his example. They can also learn gradually, by keeping up contact with him, and by understanding him better, these key points:

1 : He still feels strongly about them, even if he lives apart.
2 : He is not wholly bad (as he may have been pointed out to be), and whatever they have gained from him in terms of heredity is a mixture of good and bad also.
3 : Whatever the reasons for his departure, it cannot have been just to get away from *them*.
4 : There is no great mystery about him, which demands morbid fantasies.

The *converse* of each of these key points is met with by social workers very frequently, when they are looking into the problems of young delinquents and unhappy children who damage themselves or attempt suicide. That is to say that these children often share at least one of a set of unhealthy convictions—that they have a father who simply doesn't care (and therefore sets an example to them as well as writing them off as useless and unwanted); that they have a dark side to their character which is genetic and inescapable; that somehow the blame for the family break-up is wholly or partly due to them; and that he may be anything from a criminal to a disinherited aristocrat, whose disappearance changed everything, and who will change things again, dramatically, when he returns.

It is no good telling yourself that a normally intelligent, sensible child will not entertain such wild theories. A parent's disappearance transcends anything he is mentally equipped to deal with. This is emotional, not logical territory.

But by being around, by listening and talking, and by remaining accessible, a father can go a long way towards giving a child a more balanced view of his own worth, and of his child's own worth.

Not all children who lose all contact with one parent turn out to have serious problems. That would be a gross exaggeration. There is a tendency, however, for them to be at risk. Social workers have known this for a long time. More formal research by Joan Kelly and Judith Wallenstein shows that children in split families who maintain a link with their absent parent are distinctly more likely to have a happy, balanced, and positive outlook on what they are like and what they may achieve. There is less likelihood that they will start a criminal record, or fail in adjustment to other children or to a partner of the opposite sex.

More positively, in recent work Margaret Hennig of the Harvard Business School found that in the background of a sample of American women who had achieved success and recognition in a range of different careers there was one consistent factor—an extremely good relationship with both parents, and *particularly with the father*.

There is also evidence that keeping close to the children is good for the fathers, too. K. Rosenthal and H. Kesset analyzed the attitudes of fathers with different degrees of maintained relationship with their children: those who shared child custody in equal time with their ex-wives felt happiest in their role.

This does not stop some fathers from feeling that they might as well duck out and slip away from their children's lives. What circumstances justify this view? I believe *very few,* leaving aside the special cases where a father has a history of alcoholism and child-abuse.

Dr. G. B. Blaine, commenting on the results of long-term studies of "the children of divorce," discerned two factors which were more likely to contribute to the normal development of those children. One was an identifiable place that could be called "home." The other was the presence of an adult man and an adult woman for relatively long periods.

The research by Joan Kelly and Judith Wallenstein (which included re-visiting the same children at intervals over a number of years) pointed out clearly that *none* of the children wanted a permanent split in the family. They wanted their father around as well as their mother. They wanted very frequent visits. The most satisfied—or the ones who were the best reconciled to their situation—were those able to bicycle between the two homes. This seems to say something about children wanting to organize "access" for themselves, perhaps to check that their links are still solid with both parents, as much as it does about wanting that access and benefiting from it.

Sometimes a child gives every sign of disliking an absent parent, to the point where he becomes rude or extremely difficult to deal with whenever a visit takes place. This happened, for example, with a man called Fred who wanted to renew contact with his five-year-old son Johnny after a break of about a year. Each time Fred stood at the corner of the apartment block where he was due to meet his son, Johnny would charge across the courtyard in his direction at great speed. A few feet away Johnny would pause, declare that he was going to kill his father, and then run forward with his head lowered, aiming for the pit of Fred's stomach. Then he would try to stamp on his toes, and push him into the street. The struggling went on for several minutes, followed by a break, followed by another round of free-for-all.

These visits were tiring and rather painful for Fred. He tried deflecting Johnny's head-first onslaughts with some humor, for example with the words "I'm not a bullfighter you know!" But usually he had to put an arm-lock on his son for sheer self-protection, as well as to get away from the embarrassing scene which he was sure was being misinterpreted by all the neighbors. During the actual visits Johnny varied his behavior, but it usually included a lot of wheedling and whining and some shouts of rage—"I hate you!"—when a second ice cream was refused.

Fred wondered if it was all worthwhile. Maybe his son had really started to hate him and it was pointless pursuing their relationship any further.

But the evidence did not support this. A neighbor in the same apartment building whose son often played with Johnny, met Fred on his way to the corner of the courtyard one Saturday morning. She told him it was a nice day, and looked a bit surprised when Fred merely shook his head with a sad smile. "Why," she assured him, "you've no idea how much Johnny looks forward to your coming and boasts about it to the other kids!"

"He—he does? Really?"

"Oh, heavens yes! He tells our kid he's a dope simply because his daddy's always here, and doesn't come for him on *special visits*."

"He says that?"

"Oh yes! He told me the other day you had to come right across town to get him. Of course he thinks that's the other side of the world."

"Well. . . ."

Fred's concentration was elsewhere when Johnny made his usual lunge, so that he was badly winded when the attack was made. Winded, but rather happy, in a puzzled kind of way.

That was a few years ago. Johnny doesn't behave like a wild bull now, and the visits pass off quietly as a rule. Sometimes, still, there are moments when Johnny expresses impatience or displeasure in a physical way. He seems to need to express his negative feelings and stamping on his father's feet serves that purpose. Afterwards he is quiet, affectionate, companionable.

Time and again the very strong desires that small children have for changing what has happened and for mending the family rift become unmanageable. Frustrated because they are totally powerless and cannot really understand why their parents don't get together again, they snatch at opportunities to show how strongly they feel. They are working off the emotion which they are far too young to handle in an "adult" way. Once the emotion goes and they have made their point, they can get on with the positive side of the visit. Young children in fact are often afraid of these feelings, which increases their tension, their need to be aggressive, and to hunt for new stimulation—wheedling for ice cream, candy, presents, for this and for that. It passes: like Fred, you must be patient.

Guessing what is happening on the other side of the wall is one of the most perplexing problems of being a Saturday parent. Fred believed his child had turned against him definitively. Sometimes it is only chance remarks that help you to get an insight into what else might be going on. There was an important clue, however, that Fred overlooked: his son had developed a kind of ritual when it came to meeting him. There was a pattern to his behavior which, for one reason or another, Johnny enjoyed repeating. This doesn't happen when visits are not enjoyed. Repeated fun with a parent (even if it is rather one-sided) is a route back towards a happy understanding. You can build on something that is reliable, and a ritual provides just that. A child who is genuinely disturbed about something will often opt out of an established pattern; typically, he wants his parent to offer some compromise, and to work out what it is that is wrong so that they can get on to a better footing.

Some criticism *could* be made of the extent to which Fred tolerated bad behavior. I personally do not believe he went far wrong, although Saturday parents have a duty to help their children not to be antisocial.

But meanwhile, if you are in any doubt as to whether or not you yourself should start, or continue, to make visits to your child, then I wish you could just watch Fred and Johnny *now*.

2: What Good Does It Do?

Two people benefit greatly from frequent, regular attention: the child and the Saturday parent himself. Another person benefits marginally from it, namely the parent who is living with the child.

Some reasons why exactly this should be good for them have been outlined in Chapter 1. They should now be considered more carefully. Understanding them helps provide a framework for building up the life and habits of a Saturday parent.

How old does a child have to be before he notices (in the sense of *feels*) that his father has left the scene? Older, certainly, than if his mother moves away. But the precise age depends a great deal on the way the child has been treated, on his intelligence and personality, and particularly on the amount of contact he has had with his father. It can be as early as around his first birthday, but exceptionally it can be as late as around three.

Let us assume an average family with average people—who have slightly above-average rows. Their child is three years old, and he is an only child. He has had love and affection from both his parents. Then they split up.

To put it bluntly, the child's world is badly shaken. His confidence collapses. He may not show all of this, but he is grappling with things that he desperately wants to change. Explaining the background to him will not do very much good. He wants to deny that any change has happened. "Will everyone *please*," he is saying, "get back to normal as soon as possible?"

What can help him is to get some sense of continuation with

those people that he knows and loves. Whatever the feelings between ex-husband and ex-wife, the child's desire is for a recognizable pattern as close as possible to the one that existed before, in which everybody saw a lot of each other. Exactly *why* a young child is dependent in this way is not easy to explain. But his needs certainly go beyond the basic survival kit of food, drink, sleep and warmth. Human heredity demands more—possibly as part of an instinct that ensures biological survival and has been in human beings from their earliest days.

Very often, in the days immediately following a family split, both the adults want to make the split as complete as possible by cutting down the points of contact. The children represent a link which may be regretted, or even driven from the mind, during the heady period of dramatic reaction in which doors are slammed and vows are taken never to return. This is usually a bad time in which to try to work out a sensible scheme for allowing the absent parent to have regular access, much less to reach permanent decisions about whether to offer or to accept access to the children. Better to wait awhile, and to get help from a relative or a family friend to sound out views on an impartial basis, or to talk to someone with experience of these problems—marriage guidance counsellors, social workers, clergymen.

This can help avoid situations where one or other ex-spouse takes up a seemingly irrevocable stand. Swearing to sever all links may help you let off steam for a while, but it is not particularly adult behavior. Nor does it help the children.

Some children who are left at a very young age develop some weird interpretations of how it was that they came to have one parent missing from home. Here is a sample selection of thoughts and explanations that some children have lived with for quite a time. The worst form of fantasy is that something the child has done or failed to do somehow lies at the root of the problem.

JK is an only child, male. His father left home when he was three and hasn't been seen since. JK is married, but living apart from his wife. He is a moderately successful engineer. He has a shy personality. He enjoys life. He disliked his childhood. He rarely sees his mother.

I don't know why, but I decided my dad must have been in the army, and that he was out there, somewhere, fighting a war. I was about four or five at the time, so it didn't matter to me that there wasn't a war on at that time! I knew he *had* been in the army, so I suppose I just kept him there, in my mind. That was why he was always away. I remember looking at maps sometimes, and choosing a place, asking how it was pronounced, and then putting him there. I didn't tell my mom this, because we never talked about him. Then I remember getting into trouble once, and it made me stop thinking about him being in the army. I used to tell some kids at school he was in the army, and one day—I don't know why—I decided he had been killed in action. I was playing in one house with a couple of friends from school with toy guns and tanks and things, when one of them asked me what my dad did in the army exactly. I told him he'd been killed. Just like that. Later on, my mom looked at me very strangely, with her head on one side. She was angry. She wanted to know what I'd said about my dad. I told her I'd just said he'd been in the army and got killed—*hadn't* he? She shook her head and told me not to talk about him again. When I was older (about ten, I think), she told me little bits about him.

RB is one of two sisters who were five and seven when their parents divorced. She is a teacher and unmarried. She has suffered from a few nervous problems and allergies, now more or less overcome.

We used to make up stories about Daddy, Barbara and I. He came back at night (so we pretended to each other), and if we got things ready for a big adventure—you know, like Peter Pan or Bedknobs and Broomsticks, then he would come along and join us. I remember that if we got angry with each other, we used to say "If you're so terrible, Daddy won't come tonight." It was a sure way to reduce each other to tears, if we wanted to. We stopped playing the game when Barbara was ten and I was eight, because she said it was too childish. But sometimes, you know, we used to stay up late in our room with some food we'd smuggled up for him. It was hard to explain away sometimes, when mom heard us and came and turned on the light. . . . I can't remember how we explained to each other why he never came: it was always that he was *going* to come.

JS is the youngest of three children. His father left home when he was two. His brother and sister were then twelve and fourteen. He

ran away from home twice—the second time for good. He is unmarried, has had a succession of jobs, and is very rebellious against
officialdom, law, rules. He has some convictions but no criminal
record. He is restless, picks fights, but is popular with his friends.

> I never saw my dad at all. But my elder brother and sister told
> me about him. They used to tell me I was a pig and it was no
> wonder that dad walked out. That was when I'd done something
> to annoy them. Once he sent me a model plane, I can remember,
> and I told them he must have liked me, or he wouldn't have sent
> it to me. They just laughed.

BP is an only child. Her mother and her aunt brought her up from
about the age of four. She is unmarried. She has been visiting a
psychiatric clinic since she was fifteen for various nervous problems. She works as a clerical assistant, and is taking adult educa-
tion with the aim of a better career.

> I remembered my dad only vaguely. He was somebody that my
> mother talked about sometimes. She told me he was awful—that
> he drank too much, that he lost his temper and hit people, that he
> never gave us any money, that he smelt bad. . . . She also told
> me he had been cruel to me, although I could never remember
> this. It was only when I was seventeen that I met a teacher at
> school who had known him, and made me curious about him. I
> tracked him down in a few months and paid him a visit. He was
> very surprised to see me. We didn't know what to make of each
> other. He's old, now, and he lives alone in his apartment with a
> small dog. He hurt his back and has to move carefully. He's
> quiet and very shy. He seemed to like seeing me, but he looked
> very worried. At my third visit he told me he'd tried to see me
> when I was little, but my mom insisted that *I* didn't want to see
> *him,* and screamed every time it was suggested. He sort of mum-
> bled this, and then he looked at me as if he was afraid I would
> take offense and walk out. . . . We get on OK. I see him from
> time to time. We haven't much in common, but he's a poor old
> soul.

It is quite possible to go on and on. There are endless variations.
These examples will be enough to make two points. There is a big
difference between the first two—JK and RB—and the second two.
Few would regard the *first* two to be particularly unhappy or han-

dicapped as a result of their experiences as children. Virtually nobody regards them as such. They themselves feel a kind of deprivation, and this has affected them, although not on a scale that suggests tragedy. The *second* two are distinctly worse off. Both of these have had recurrent crises in their personal lives. Most people would regard them as people with problems, who need help.

Presenting brief snapshots of people in this way inevitably leads to simplification. Of course there are other factors, apart from absent parents, that have affected them, sometimes for better, sometimes for worse. But there is a significant distinction between the two pairs. The first two developed rich fantasies about their fathers. This satisfied a need when they were young, but it had to come to an end. Gradually, they had to be introduced to the reality, as opposed to the fantasy, and to learn to live with it. In this they were partially, not wholly successful. One had help from his mother and the sisters seem to have helped each other. The second two people were *fed* fantasies that they could not live with. One is scarred by the fear that he may have been responsible, to some extent, for his parents' split. He realizes that his brother and sister were simply venting their feelings against him in a rather cruel fashion. He realizes it in a logical way but he still cannot live with it, or with the idea that there may be a kernel of truth behind their comments. The young woman was given what she is now convinced was a distorted picture of anything that her father could have been like. She could not live with it, because it was too near: what she was told about was something horrible *in the family,* and therefore *in her.* Neither of these two seems to have enjoyed much help from others who were close to them to get a better perspective on what had happened, and to make the best of what they had.

Not everyone gets on well with their children—or with their parents, for that matter. This is worth underlining, since there is obviously no guarantee that simply if you see your children all will be rosy. But surely it is better to give yourself the *chance* of success. Here are two examples where contact was maintained through childhood. In neither case does the person who is talking have any obvious problem that has seriously affected his life. There *is* evidence, however, of deriving lasting benefit from contact with an absent parent. The benefit is very different, but still impressive.

The first account is taken from an interview with a woman who admired her father a lot.

LM is in her early twenties, unmarried, a university graduate. She has made a successful start in a business career. She is popular, and has a wide range of interests, including sports and charity work. She has a very confident manner and a strong personality and she expresses herself easily with people.

> I always had a good time when I saw my dad. It wasn't what we did so much, as just getting out to see him and picking up again. I used to scrounge candy and ice cream off him like mad, and there were times I remember saying we had to do *this*, or we had to see that film. It's embarrassing now, thinking about it! But he had a lot of patience, I suppose, and he was good-humored about it—even when he said "No" very loud. He could always make me laugh. It was good seeing him just to get me out of one of my black moods. The weekends when he came I looked forward to, because I knew that whatever was going wrong at school we could talk about, and he would help me. This was much easier than with mom, although of course I love my mom very much.
>
> Some things were easier to talk about with mom—I guess you can imagine what—but there were other things I wanted to talk to *him* about. Like my mom's second husband, for instance. We just don't get on. Dad gave me some good advice about how to be tactful, and I needed that.
>
> Now he's in hospital, and it's me who has to go and see *him*. I owe him a lot, because thanks to him I always had two parents, even if they were divorced.

The man who gave the interview summarized below had a very different view of his father. PS is in his late twenties and lives with his partner and child. A successful union organizer, he is politically committed. He is respected as a leader, although "loved *and* hated."

> I was very competitive with my father. If he showed me how to do something one way, I'd always try to find some other way, just to be different. We argued a lot, and we didn't always get along. When I was thirteen or fourteen, I remember, I used to criticize just about everything he said.
>
> But it was always better if he was there. Sometimes I didn't

see him for a month or two, and my brother tells me I was terrible to live with because I used to take it out on everyone else. Whatever plans he had for taking me out I used to argue with, but it was always much better if he came than if he didn't come. When I was seventeen I decided I'd had enough of him and his bourgeois ideals. I pulled out from home, too. Too cosy, too stuffy . . . I see them sometimes now. They're OK, but they're boring and they never change. You need parents when you're young, I believe that. It was good for me to see both of them, that's for sure. Then you've just got to live your own life.

Both of these people—who are about as different in their outlook as possible—share a conviction that life is worth living, and that they are going to do something good in it. They see the opportunities rather than the problems. It scarcely matters that one wants to work within the social context in which she has developed, while the other intends changing it radically. Both have ideals, both are active, and both are confident. Their parents each had something to contribute to the way they progressed. It is difficult to imagine them being *quite* the same if they had lacked one or other of these influences.

Whether PS would admit to his father's being an influence is problematical. But he feels he gained from his attention and help. It is also noteworthy that PS appears to set himself strict standards as a father: he spends a lot of time with his own child. His family is unconventional but very close. He gives the impression that he is applying some important things that he has been shown, while being very critical of social requirements that are simply there "for show."

If you are convinced that there is some good you can do as a Saturday parent, it is worth considering some things that you can *not* achieve this way.

First and foremost, it has to be recognized that you are one of two parents; and that the *other* parent has closer contact. Nothing is going to change that. The chances of becoming the guiding influence in your child's life are relatively small, however desirable you may think that would be. Look at it from your child's point of view. Your child's attitude towards the family split is virtually bound to be one of regret, and this continues even if there is understanding of the causes at an intellectual level. You are the person who has pulled out; the less predictable parent; the one who might not like him (or her); the object, perhaps, of recurrent criticism in terms of money, housing conditions, social opportunities, or in terms of whatever hangover from the divorce court may still exist. This is a formidable handicap for your image.

Some Saturday parents suspect this but make a key mistake. They feel that by struggling directly against their "image problem" they will somehow regain mastery, or the central point of affection in their child's mind. Almost inevitably, they fail.

Any attack on loyalty to the parent who has stayed with the child is taken as *confirming* a point of view. It may simply fit in with the picture that has been painted at home, that is, it just goes to show that this person cannot be trusted and is always predisposed to attack. It gives the child further evidence of the split between father and mother. Whenever such hostilities are reopened, there is renewal of regret.

What *is* worth fighting for is building positive links; inspiring the feeling that with you any questions may be asked, any advice asked, and any help sought. You cannot do this by frontal assault. Attacking another's influence is pointless if you are not seen to have anything solid to offer in exchange.

You have to be seen and judged on your child's terms. You have to be a good person to meet regularly, a person why tries to be helpful and who is fun to be with. When your child reaches adolescence, he or she will—like all others—make a number of basic choices about their future relationships with adults they have known. There is no obligation to live with or even see *any* parent once one is sixteen, and with a suddenness that alarms many people, independence is declared. That is what may happen in your case, whether you like it or not. The only sensible precaution, if you want to maintain contact with your child up to and beyond that point, is to *be* somebody worth knowing. The following table contrasts what is counterproductive with what actually works.

One of the other pitfalls to avoid can be summed up by saying that if you haven't got time to spend with your child you can't expect to make up for it with money.

There are plenty of examples of parents who feel they have not been visiting enough, or have not made themselves available for

AVOID	AIM AT
Arguing directly against whatever the other parent has been saying.	Listening to what your child has to say, and taking a friendly interest.
Trying to pull the other parent down in your child's estimation.	Answering questions in a way that expands conversation, i.e., without laying down the law.
Trying to persuade your child that your view of everything is the right one.	Noticing any problems, where you might be able to help.
Reacting defensively at any hint of criticism from child or other parent.	Being around, on a dependable, reliable basis.
Preaching any particular religious, moral or social doctrines that you know are contradictory to the home views.	Showing that you have your own standards and that, even if these are different from those at home, at least you are consistent.
Trying to solve your problems through your child.	Enjoying time together, rather than treating it as an opportunity to impress or persuade.

talking things over. They want to make up for it, but contact has been broken and there are two big obstacles in the way of re-establishing it: there isn't the time, and it's difficult to communicate. These parents put their trust in physical objects—train sets, bicycles or cold cash. Normally objects are chosen instead of money, since there is then the chance of telling oneself, "Each time he looks at it, he'll think of me." Sheer self-deception. It's often a nasty moment when an absent parent asks how his child is enjoying the expensive toy he sent at Christmas—only to find out that there has been a complete loss of memory as to what came from that source.

What a child actually learns in these circumstances is a long way from what a parent expects. It's nothing like "Here's a marvelous parent, who is so generous with his gifts, and so thoughtful about getting me nice things." It's more like "Here's a soft touch whenever I need something new."

It makes sense really. If you treat your son or daughter in such a way that money and possessions take the place of communication, why shouldn't he or she get exactly that idea, and try it out on *you?*

RO found that his children—with whom he had not lived for several years—smiled and said "Thank you." But that was as far as it went.

> I didn't have much money when I left them. I sent what I could, but if I wanted to see the kids I was always asked for more than I had. So I packed it in. I saw them off and on, but more off than on. Then my luck changed. They were twelve and thirteen by this time, and I tried hard to get along with them. Money wasn't a problem any more. But trying to talk to them, or get them to talk to me, or get them to see me as a friend who wants to help. . . .
>
> I bought them some pretty good things. Asked them what they wanted, and they told me. When they got the idea, they wrote to me or telephoned and said what they wanted. Only it was always difficult to meet—either they couldn't make it or I couldn't. Then I came to my senses and found they were mercenary little buggers who looked on me as a real-life Santa Claus.

Eventually RO changed his tactics. It hasn't always worked and it hasn't always been perfect. For a while he had to be very patient. When they realized that a telephone call from their father was not to ask what they wanted to be given next, but was just a conversation with casual questions and answers, and an exchange of information and feelings, his children became rather cold and seemed to have little time for him. But, in the end, they met and talked, and began to understand each other more. Children do that, unless there is a really big emotional barrier. They admire persistence, and they appreciate somebody trying to get through to them.

There was one mistake that RO *could* have made, but didn't. When parents suddenly come to their senses and find that they are being exploited for money and possessions, they sometimes have recourse to bargaining. For example, "OK, you can have your skateboard, but you've got to come over here and collect it. We'll have a couple of hours together, right? You'll be getting lunch as well, remember."

This can win you more face-to-face confrontation. But it fails to establish any kind of long-term relationship. Long-term friends don't have to bargain for each other's company. By using words like those quoted above, you are yourself descending to the mercenary level. You are setting a value on the time you have together, in terms of presents, etc. The message gets through that this is how you personally put prices on things like friendship.

In this as in many other ways, your children will reflect your own values, just as you reveal them.

Tokens of affection, then, are not enough. They are simply ways of purchasing relief from guilt, or of avoiding the problems and anxiety of getting together. Trying to buy your way into your children's esteem establishes the wrong basis for meaningful contact. There is no substitute for being seen, making yourself available, and looking for interests that your children and you will enjoy sharing.

One question which is in many an absent parent's mind (but which many are too nervous about to come to grips with) is this: If I keep up contact with my children, will they continue to love me, and to want to be like me, *despite* the presence of a stepfather (or stepmother) now or in the future?

It's an uncomfortable thought. It's not enough to say this is something you should have thought about before you split up the home. The natural impulse is towards influencing your child, and towards keeping the bond intact. Nobody likes the idea of a "stranger" coming into the child's life, usurping the authority role, siphoning off the affection, molding the future adult. However much you try to be objective or fair-minded—as in "The newcomer's got to have a fair deal"—at a deeper level you resent the intrusion and the greater opportunity that the intruder has for enjoying your children's company.

I believe that it is worthwhile recognizing these feelings for what they are, rather than trying to cover them up with platitudes. That way you are less likely to sound sour or snide when this person comes up in conversation with your children. Any such tone is quickly noticed. It may make them anxious, it may confirm some of their fears, and it certainly is not calculated to make them happy. Once again they sense that they are cast in the role of the rope between two tug of war teams.

The point of this is that your goal in securing and maintaining contact with your children, as a Saturday parent, is going to be unrealistic if you visualize it as a battle against the influence of your ex-wife, or of some other person. You are in no position, in fact, to win any more major battles. Are battles really worthwhile?

In rare instances, for example, when one of these people turns out to be a criminal, yes, you will need to observe carefully what is happening, enlist expert advice and fight. But generally speaking families and children thrive on peace.

In your case, your child may have the opportunity to enjoy seeing four people who have each got different gifts to offer. He can benefit from knowing the different ways of each person in each of two pairs. He will be introduced to a wider range of subjects, points of view and behavior than a child in a so-called "normal" family. The positive side is there, too, as well as the unpleasant feelings that your child went through during the divorce period. Your child has a right to that positive side, and all that it can bring.

But in one important way, it is *you* who matters. A child cannot start to look on the bright side of things if he senses rejection or neglect.

You may have made an unsuccessful marriage. But you have it in you to make a very successful divorce.

3 : "My, How You've Changed..."

Children never stand still. No matter how fixed an idea you may have as a parent that your child is basically the same person from week to week, subtle changes are happening all the time. Half of these changes parents barely notice even if they are living together. Some of the other changes take a parent by surprise, especially when they are *not* living together.

The parent who lives with his child has the advantage of watching him develop in a gradual way. This is not simply because it is a day-to-day experience as opposed to the weekly or bi-monthly meetings of the parent who lives apart. It is also a matter of being able to observe reactions at different times of day, and in different circumstances—at meals, with friends, in front of visitors, when meeting strangers—and in different moods. Living with his child a parent knows only too clearly the changes that take place between a happy day and a sad day, what he is like when he gets excited, disappointed, moody, puzzled, tired. . . . The evidence, in other words, which helps a parent realize that his child is developing in particular ways is fuller and richer if the parent is there most of the time.

The parent who is not around tends to rely on snapshots in time to form his impressions. Because it is so often a set scene that they play through together when they meet, there is a sense of habit in the minds of both parent and child at this time unless, of course, access has been very sporadic. The two of you have your parts to

28

play at this set scene, important parts, which you appreciate, but which frequently do not have time to reflect all that has been happening off-stage in the background.

It is different if your child is in the habit of making contact whenever it suits *him,* telephoning and asking to come over for a visit, or just dropping in. Where this kind of free and easy contact exists, you enjoy a better chance of noticing what progress has been made, or what behavioral problems may be in the offing. These circumstances are still comparatively unusual, although the trend may be towards them.

In most cases access still has to be agreed upon and arranged at mutually convenient times by both the parents, perhaps through an intermediary. The meeting is then organized more as an *event* than as a straightforward continuation of normal life. You and your child each prepare yourselves. Both of you are apt to develop particular patterns of behavior for it. This varies with the age of the child, of course, and his personality. It can be rather different when there is more than one child. But over and above these differences, both parent and child want to have a predictable, stable and comforting time during the event. The easiest way to ensure this is to give the meetings a pattern, and to adopt the same mood for them, as consistently as possible. During your intervening lives, perhaps, there has been too much change: when you see each other, you want to hold on to something that is firm.

But then there are these changes that are happening all the time. In the end the gap between how your child regularly acts at the special visit and what he really feels, what his real interests are, and how he views the separation situation, becomes so great that an emotional outburst takes place. Usually, the child himself has very little control over this. He is in a conflict: part of him wants to go on enjoying the visits in their comfortable routine, which reassure him about an important dimension in his make-up; another part is questioning a lot of things that he used to take for granted. It may be extremely hard for him, all of a sudden, not to spend more of his free time with his friends. He may need to be near a particular friend, depending on the stage he has reached. Children who are emotionally more mature may be able to weave a neat course for themselves between two such conflicting demands; but this is more rare than not realizing why they are feeling different, and not being able to cope happily with the conflict.

In some cases the outburst is in the open. There is an alarming switch into bad behavior during the visit. Your child may do things he knows you dislike for no apparent reason. Also in this category comes a break in agreeing to having the visit at all. There may come one day a blunt refusal to meet you. A less obvious outburst, but one which is no less real, is when mysterious headaches and other illnesses—sometimes with very clear symptoms—intervene to prevent the visits from taking place.

It is all too easy, when this kind of thing happens, to look for a simple explanation in terms of something disconcerting that may have happened that day or the previous week. "You must have said something to upset him," is the kind of accusation that seems all too logical for the parents to make, whether it is thrown at one side or the other. What may in fact have been happening is a major change in outlook that would have been obvious to anyone watching the child regularly, but which would escape the notice of someone who only saw his well-rehearsed behavior every other Saturday.

Here are a few examples of change that arrived so suddenly that it took both parts of the split family by surprise. These are followed by an analysis of some of the common patterns of change that children often go through. If you know about them, it is much easier for you to be on the lookout for signs that will help you realize when you should adapt your approach, and why.

Sandra

Sandra is now in her early twenties. When her parents separated, she was eight. She seemed to enjoy the visits from her father every two weeks and the outings that went with them. She showed no signs of wanting to avoid him.

What they did during these visits varied from season to season, and according to the weather. In summer they might go to a swimming pool, or to the zoo, and end up with a hamburger. On a colder Saturday they might go to a museum or movie, or else stay for a couple of hours with her father's sister, playing Monopoly or watching TV.

They chatted easily (most times) and there were very few problems over behavior to sour the afternoon. If they argued about anything, it was usually over the number of ice creams she should have in the space between twelve and six, or the kind of present she might expect at Christmas. Few normal families would be without some arguments like these.

She asked him questions sometimes, such as "How are you getting along now Daddy?," and he would talk a bit about his apartment and his work. He asked her about her school, her pet dog, and her dancing lessons, and was usually assured that "everything's fine!" They were affectionate to each other: Sandra used to give her father a big kiss at the start and at the end of each visit, and usually contrived to be carried by him some time during the day. But they never got particularly close to each other's thoughts and they hardly ever talked about any real problems. When Sandra was about eleven and a half, she began to feel a kind of anxiety about these visits shortly before they were due to happen. In her own words:

> For about a year or so, I hated the idea of going out with my father. What was so strange was that when we were actually with each other, I felt fine. But beforehand I would have sick headaches, or I used to plead with Mommy that it was time we visited Grandma. I tried everything. And I was *really* sick, you know.

Her father recalls this period very clearly, too:

> At first I thought that Margaret—my ex-wife—was trying to put a stop to my visiting. She told me on the phone, or when I came to the front door, that Sandra was suddenly ill or too upset to see me. And yet I *knew* we'd had good times together. When it got more and more difficult, and I was seeing her less and less often, I suspected this was a way of getting me right out of the picture.

He saw his lawyer, who advised him to treat everyone as calmly as he could; to avoid asking Sandra directly about any pressure from her mother to refuse to come; to try to arrange to have visits at different days and times, so that they would not be so predictable; to keep trying to see Sandra, and to report back if things did not get gradually better.

He tried to follow this guidance. But he found he had to ask

Sandra, as casually as he could, when they were walking across the park one afternoon: "By the way, Sandra, does your Mommy not like you coming out with me any more?"

She looked apprehensive, and mumbled that "She doesn't mind."

He did not know what to make of this, and felt he should not pursue it. They had not much experience of sharing deep feelings.

Suspicion was not limited to one side. Sandra remembers that her mother looked at her very seriously one Saturday morning—when she had protested that her cold and sore throat were too bad to allow her out of doors with her father—and asked her, "What does he do that you don't like?" When she hung her head, this was followed by, "Come on, you can tell Mommy." Sandra cannot remember what she replied—only that she was embarrassed.

Several changes had been going on that nobody was coming to terms with. First, Sandra was on the verge of puberty, and was unclear about what was happening to her, and about how she should react to her father. She continued being affectionate and demonstrative with him, because this was the established pattern. But it felt wrong somehow. She wanted to stop romping with him, and be a different person in his eyes. She could see that many of her friends were becoming rather different individuals, who were affectionate in a more mature way, with reserve. It was indeed hard to see how she should develop her relationship with her father, whom she saw regularly, but briefly, in a stereotyped setting.

Then there was the question of allegiance, which had never really bothered her before. When she was younger, she had no problem about enjoying herself one way with mother, another way with father. She recollects that during this earlier period she told her friends at school how lucky she was having two birthday treats, on Friday with her mother and on Saturday with her father. The rights and wrongs of the separation she had never explored much, and this had not been encouraged. She regretted her father's leaving, and sometimes wondered why he should have done so.

Now that she was older, she realized that this had been a split involving pain and bitterness. In fact, it was clear that there was still pain and bitterness around. Before, it had been much easier to have it both ways. At eleven, the question of right and wrong made her distinctly uncomfortable about shifting from one side to the other every two weeks. Nothing was more natural than that her mother, with whom she had always lived, and had been close and loving, should be the one who was "right," as opposed to "wrong." Sandra was feeling more strongly, as she became more like a woman, that this was the side to which she belonged. The genuine delight which she could still feel when with her father became a source of guilt. Without knowing exactly why, her mind and her body were trying to organize her out of the visits, to remove the guilty feelings.

Another kind of change affecting Sandra was not so much a set of attitudes as a new need. Most of her friends shared the activities she enjoyed. But they could plan those activities on Saturday afternoons knowing that they could count on being there, irrespective of visits. Sandra made appointments, arrangements to meet, to do things together, because she wanted to be with these people; she broke the appointments, because every now and then she had to. The other advantage they had was simply being able to hang about and meet each other. This is an event which parents often disregard as having no real educational or entertainment function. But it is what young teenagers love to do—an apparently purposeless loafing which sometimes seems to be no more than sitting on a wall, discussing what things they *might* be doing—if only it wasn't raining, or they had more time, or money, or different friends around them. Sometimes it is communicating with each other by playing music that each recognizes and feels is closer to *them* than to those of another generation. In fact, they are exploring each other's feelings and responses and finding out how they resemble and how they are different from each other. They do this casually, gradually.

There was no inspired teacher who stepped in and explained everything, showing each person in this case history how to make things easier for him- or herself, and for everyone else. Some of it became more obvious later on. Meanwhile, Sandra went through almost a year of making it hard for herself and her father to get together. This was followed by a gap of six months, during which she refused outright to have anything to do with him. Christmas brought a partial reconciliation, but she was well into her fourteenth year before she accepted once again that they should meet every so often. This did not mean that her basic allegiance was affected. Nor, now, was it a case of repeating a pattern without having any control over it. If she planned something with her friends, she telephoned her father and changed the date; and sometimes she arranged to have a friend with her when she met him. On his part, he took to writing to her with a special idea for doing something together, if he felt she might enjoy it. Before long they went away together for a week's holiday.

When her father remarried, Sandra was fifteen. She readily made friends with his new wife.

Since that time they have kept in touch with each other informally but fairly regularly. Sandra is training to be a nurse, and lives in a residence. She is interested in what she is doing, has a wide circle of friends, and strikes the interviewer as being a very balanced person. When she talks about the difficulties of the 11–13 period, she feels that puberty and concern for her mother were the main factors that affected her, drawing her away from her father. But she accepts that the other points suggested above might have played some part. She is very grateful to her father for trying to get through to her when she was at her most forbidding. "Looking back, I don't know how he had the patience to keep asking if he could take me out. I don't think *I* would have gone on for so long without encouragement. I'm glad he did, though, now."

Brian

Brian is now eighteen. When he was nine, his parents separated. His father bought season tickets for the football games, and used to take Brian along. Brian remarked:

> It was strange, sometimes. I wanted to know a lot more about him. There usually wasn't much time to talk before the kick-off, because we had to cross the town in a crowded subway, and then get a bus to the ground. I used to work out questions I could ask him at half-time—about where he lived, what he was doing, and what he did when he sometimes went up north. Sometimes I got a bit of an answer when we were eating chocolate, or lining up for the john. But I was always puzzled about him.

Apparently Brian's father was not very talkative, and rather nervous when replying to questions. "I think now he was trying to be nice—trying not to say anything that would upset me, or that I might repeat at home, and cause a row. He was much happier when talking about our team's chances of winning, anyway."

In fact, Brian was not all that keen on football. He attended largely, on his own admission, out of duty and habit. The obligation became strained when he wanted more time with his friends. The breaking-point came one day when he decided that his mother was very hard done by.

> I found her crying one morning, and she told me she just didn't know where next week's food was going to come from. She had been working part-time, but now the office was closed down. I told her—I was eleven years old then—that I'd tell Dad when I next saw him that he had to give us more money. She told me not to say anything, but she was obviously bitter about him. I decided to tell him anyway. It seemed easy at first, but at the game it wasn't so easy.

At half-time, he blurted out that there wasn't very much money at home. "I wish I could help," was his father's answer. There was an embarrassing silence with neither knowing what to say.

In the weeks that followed, Brian developed the habit of saying as little as he possibly could. His father asked him if he still enjoyed football, and Brian replied, "Not much." For a time they discussed—sometimes on the telephone, sometimes face-to-face—whether they should meet the following Saturday, and what they might do. Whatever his father suggested, Brian shrugged, and said something like "I suppose so."

"I never actually said to him I didn't want to go out with him anymore. I expect I just froze him out."

The contact ceased, Brian's father deciding apparently that they simply could not hit it off successfully any more. Brian's mother remarried, and he later found that his father had done the same, and had moved away. He hasn't seen him since he was eleven. He regrets it.

"I must have been very difficult for him to deal with," Brian admits now. "I learnt that he never had much money to rub together himself, anyway. But I resented him. I didn't know any better. And he didn't want to tell me.''

Brian sums up his father as someone who wanted to be nice, but did not really know how. There were times when he, Brian, wanted to meet again, but he didn't know exactly how to go about this, tactfully. "I didn't want to be bored by football again, either," he admits.

He likes to feel that some day he may track his father down, and say hello.

This looks like another example of a separated parent being unprepared for dealing with change. Whether he would have been more perceptive and imaginative about keeping close to his son if he had still been at home is open to question. But being apart must have made it all the more difficult to act appropriately.

The crisis in Brian's home over money seems to have forced the issue, so that Brian took his mother's side in a more clear-cut and resentful way than might have been the case. From the outside, it seems as if his father's refusal to discuss money in any detail is to his credit, if the alternative would have been a heated argument. But saying nothing at all doesn't really help anyone. If he had recognized the change in his son's outlook and emotional state, he would have adjusted his discretion, perhaps, to making his position clear, to asking about the situation at home, to saying that he had his problems but perhaps they could work something out. This is hard to write, because no one knows exactly what the man's circumstances were. But Brian knows now that he was earning little, and that he supported his family right up to Brian's mother's remarriage; he must have had something to say for himself in his defense. His son was at an age when he wanted to dig a little into his father's ways of thinking and his ideals. Seeing him once a week at football in an entirely predictable context was a poor substitute.

Another change that can take both parents by surprise may occur during the 14–16 period. During these years, some teenagers find it distinctly harder than others to work out what kind of person they want to be, and what kind they want to be *seen* to be. They cannot decide on what they think is right, or desirable. Sometimes a parent can take note of this agonizing indecision by observing conscious efforts on the part of a teenager to dress, talk and be like x or y—

sometimes for as long as two weeks on end. This can affect any young person—however many of his parents he is living with.

But when one parent is absent, some teenagers feel like changing their life stance completely—often persuaded by embarrassment or a failure of some kind—and they feel a compulsion to check out that other parent. It is as though they were seeking a clue long denied them as to what they should be doing, and how they should gain the poise and the peace of mind that has been eluding them. What secret has she (or he) got that failed to get passed on after the split? What they are looking for exactly, they cannot usually say. Probably they want another chance to make sure about the attitudes they have picked up, and the aims they are pursuing. Often they talk about 'not being understood' at home and try to change homes, in case they have been in the wrong one all along.

This can obviously create problems for both parents and increase their mutual suspicion.

Alice
Alice recalls:

> I must have seemed like a yo-yo when I was fifteen. The first time I left was when I'd had a screaming match with my mother about coming home late from parties. I felt I was the only girl for miles around who was stuck with a mom who came out of the ark. I hated school at the time too. One evening I turned up at my dad's place, and said I was staying. Didn't give him much chance!
>
> He had his girl friend living there at the time. It wasn't easy for him, because at first she and I just glared at each other.

A month later she was back with her mother, convinced that she had made a mistake. She was not "understood" at her father's home, either. He too, it seemed, needed to be given some sort of notice about intentions to be in or out for meals. He objected to taking over responsibility for her without being told what she intended doing in the evenings and when she would be back. Moreover, she found she could not monopolize his attention, to talk seriously.

She went home, and set about cheering her mother up. But the two of them started to fight again.

I made three long visits to my father that year. The last one was the best. We'd got to know each other better by then. In fact, we went off on our holidays with Sarah (his girl friend). It sounds like a recipe for disaster. But we got along fine. I'd never expected Sarah to be able to help me, but we talked for hours together, and at the end of the holiday I felt far more mature and less selfish. Now and then she'd tell me to get out of their hair, but I didn't mind that. When I got back, I felt relaxed, and took things much more easily.

Alice went back to live with her mother for another year, before moving out to share an apartment with friends. This was a much quieter year, during which she simply abandoned the unequal struggle against subjects she did not expect to pass exams in and concentrated on getting some basics for a secretarial course. Freedom became less of an issue, because she had learnt something about compromise and was planning for complete independence in the near future. Her mother meanwhile had rejected direct confrontation as pointless if she were going to maintain contact with her daughter.

Now that Alice *is* independent, with her own family, it is interesting that she sees each of her parents about as much as the other. This averages out at about once a month. Neither can be said to have "won" or "lost"; both needed to contribute to the formation of the adult Alice.

During her "mad year," as she calls it, she needed to explore the other half of her make-up at close quarters, in order to find out:

> why she was getting into so many difficulties;
> why she could not maintain harmony with her mother;
> how much she should fight for her own ways of doing things, and how far she should fit in with others;
> what it was that she might be good at, as opposed to the problem areas in which she merely attracted criticism.

If these are read out of the context of a case history, they are remarkably like *adult* questions; plenty of adults have no idea how to answer them for themselves. Alice had reached this position without, apparently, her father noticing. If he had known about this change, he might have been forewarned that the occasional outing with polite chit-chat was no longer enough for Alice, and that she might even turn up unexpectedly on his doorstep.

There was also, one can imagine, a long-term build-up of curiosity about her father and about what life was like in his home. What did it feel like there? What did everybody *do?* Was it as sinful as her mother had implied? Did part of her belong in this different atmosphere? What would *she* be like in it?

The grass often seems greener on the other side of the fence. When it proves to have brown patches in it, just like the grass you know, the vacillation that caused Alice to change homes six times in twelve months is a very possible result.

A parent who is "abandoned" by the child in the way that Alice's mother was is sometimes heard to complain that life in the other home seems richer, more glamorous, and that an impressionable teenager is easily bought with money. No doubt this sometimes contributes to switching homes. But most such teenagers have questions that they have been unable to answer; they are curious about differences in living, rather than wanting to roam round a department store with a credit card.

The final comment on Alice's sixteenth year is that throughout this time her younger brother (then twelve) used to meet his father regularly, nearly every two weeks, seemingly oblivious of any problems in the background, and without any desire to change or do different things. He knew that his sister had had scenes with both parents, but he shrugged his shoulders. *He* valued quiet continuity and, to give them credit, everyone respected this and helped him to get it. In part, his was a different personality. Very possibly his father had a better rapport, and a better instinctive understanding of what he was like and what he expected from the separated parent. But at the same time he was at a different *stage,* from the point of view of the likelihood of change.

When thinking about how children change from the point of view of *access,* it is impossible not to think first about their changing feelings with regard to *separation.* By definition, separation is the state (occasionally the process) within which access is arranged. Separation is affecting them all the time. Access can influence the effects, but it does not alter the fact of separation.

Below a certain age, a father may have made too little or too infrequent an impact on a very young child for separation to be understood or appreciated for what it is. Up till about two a child feels much more concern about mother being sad or anxious—which communicates itself extremely easily to a very young mind—than about the absence of the man who played with him occasionally, carried him around and was identified as "Daddy" (by an early talker), but not as someone who was crucial to the family world.

Often in the third year (but it can be later, depending on how close the family is and how perceptive the child is) there is a gradual attachment to the father that makes a child anxious about him if he is away only briefly on a business trip. If he disappears altogether, there is at first a denial of this. The child is stubborn about continuing to ask when he is going to return, however clearly he is told this will not happen any more. Slowly, there is a kind of unwilling acceptance of the new state of things, and grief.

When it is the mother who leaves, the timing is completely different. Many authorities recommend that if a child is to be adopted this should be fixed up in his first two months, to avoid emotional and behavioral problems that may set in when a perplexed infant loses his mainstay. They base this on observations from many studies. When a young child of practically *any* age is left by his mother, there is a risk of serious grief and emotional difficulty. If he is six or more, he is still going to regret the loss very deeply, but the effect on him may not be *quite* as severe; and so on, as he gets older.

But to get back to the more usual situation. When the father leaves the home, there is a change in both the extent and the way in which a child is affected that becomes more obvious from the age of about five upwards. This can be very roughly summarized as the difference in emphasis between anxiety that the roof is caving in and concern for the quality of life after it has done so. The child may still be prone to denying the fact of separation. But he now has much more equipment which he can use to come to terms with it: he has more vocabulary, more experience at exchanging thoughts, so he can talk more about what is happening that is important to him. When you can describe something you do not necessarily gain control over it, but at least you can give a shape to it and keep it within bounds. Gradually, you can adjust to it.

Table 2 compares the reactions that are typical of particular age groups when a parent leaves home with the child's attitudes towards visits, and the changing needs that go with them. The two sets of reactions are interrelated—although this can be obscured sometimes by the shock that usually affects children for some time after the moment of a family split, which of course may arrive at *any* age.

The attitudes of a child below seven are likely to be very confused. His wishes are often stronger than the ability to observe what is really going on and to act accordingly. In most young children, in most families, there is a very strong wish for the separation to stop and for the whole family unit to knit together again. Sometimes the child *seems* to understand what is being carefully explained to him. But he will be on the look-out for any sign of a return to what he regards as normal. This means he will misinterpret comments: a remark like "Let's go back to Mommy now" at the end of a visit is understood to mean "We're now going back home, and I'm coming back to stay." When events prove the young listener wrong, he is resentful, and may try to spoil any arrangements by being obstructive, naughty, or tearful. He is, in the language of today, "disturbed." But how far he looks or acts "disturbed" will vary greatly. It is worth remembering that it is only too easy to give a false hope to someone at this age, which contributes to unhappiness.

Tony and Tim

Tony and Tim provide an interesting contrast between the outlook of two of the age groups that have been discussed. Tony is nearly six, while Tim is just three. About a year ago their parents broke up. They are visited by their father fairly regularly and they have a good time together. Tim has been told often enough that his father is *his* father: but he invariably refers to him as "Tony's dad." "What are you going to do today, Tim?" "We're going off to see Tony's dad." He was too young, at the split, for this man to acquire a personal meaning as his own father. But he has heard Tony often talking to "Dad," and he probably senses a very close link between the two in the way Tony addresses him and talks about him.

TABLE 2
Reactions When a Parent Leaves

Age of child	Mother leaves	Father leaves	Key reactions to visits from the non-custodial parent
Under 2 months	May notice very little.	Notices nothing.	
Up to 2½ yrs	Emotional and behavioral problems of varying severity.	May notice very little.	Uncomplicated pleasure, unless the visit is associated with anxiety on the part of the resident parent. Concern over long gaps away from mother (over half a day) unless routine.
From 2½ to 6 yrs	Sense of major change, loss of focal point. Strong tendency to deny the fact of separation, turning to resentment, bitterness. Concern over personal responsibility for "driving parent away."	Sense of change—which is major if the family has been very close. Tendency to vary between apparent acceptance of separation and belief that it is only temporary. Increased dependence on mother.	Pleasure, becoming dependent on some kind of regular contact with absent parent. Reassurance needed about acceptance by that parent. Seeking for tokens of affection, approval. Attempts to delay departure at end of visit or to inspire reconciliation.

From 6 to 9 yrs	Sadness is persistent. Tends to be hard to amuse except superficially. Worry about continuation of normal life; about stability of what they know and need.	Sadness. Some clinging to mother. Search for compensation in possessions, and/or activities. Some alternation between acceptance and hope of re-unification.	Pleasure, continued need for regularity of contact, and increased demand for tokens-presents, etc. Some "paying back" of the absent parent through rough behavior or disobedience. Curiosity about that parent's life. No conflict over double standard: pro-mother and pro-father in turn.
From 9 to 14 yrs	Sense of loss, but emotional response tied to nature of relationship with mother. Girls vary from boys. Daughters depend on friends of same sex outside home, or resent their puberty strongly. Boys may gravitate more towards their father.	Sense of loss; emotional response varies (as when mother leaves). Sex differences here too: girls may become suspicious of or reject the male sex, while boys may feel less confident socially (since they have been rejected as companions).	Pleasure in visits varies according to degree of blame attached to absent parent, and to sense of rejection. Pattern of visits may be challenged. Some preference for company of own close friends—but no real break wanted for long with the absent parent. Relationship has to develop; more compromise needed.

TABLE 2 (*Continued*)
Reactions When a Parent Leaves

Age of child	Mother leaves	Father leaves	Key reactions to visits from the non-custodial parent
From 14 to 16 yrs	Depending on maturity, they take a more realistic view. But an immature teenager, with puberty problems, and/or social self-doubt, may interpret the event as underlining his own inadequacy.	Depends on how close they have been, e.g. on how far a son has been modelling himself on his father (consciously or not), and how far a daughter has been depending on his response as approval of her femininity.	Success becomes increasingly dependent on having mutual interests and enjoying each other's company *as such*, i.e. not just because of the blood connection. Where less blame is attached, children sometimes revert to the "double standard" of the 6–9 period.

When the time comes for the two of them to be taken back to their mother, there are often tears from Tony—but not so often from Tim. Recently Tony asked if his father would be coming on holidays with them (together with their mother). His tone *expected* the answer "Yes," although the separation has been logically explained to him more than once. Wishes are stronger than logic.

One week a child like Tony will feel happy with what he has been doing and will seem to accept the situation maturely. The next week, perhaps after a heavy cold or a bad time at school, the world looks more gloomy and his wish to reunite the family and gain comfort from reunion looms larger in his mind. His temper suffers. He may shout, "I never want to come out with you again!" But he doesn't mean it. What he is getting at is that he hates the split, and this is a vivid way of expressing that.

Sometimes he senses that both his parents are attentive for signs of "disturbance," and he may display some of these if he feels it will draw them together, quite apart from the more obvious point that he is flagging attention to himself as someone who needs help.

Later, there is a period between seven and ten when there is a much steadier adjustment to the separation. He will regret it from time to time, but there will be long stretches during which the ordinary distractions of life are engrossing enough to keep him from brooding over the way his family has divided. Visits are welcomed, as a rule, and there is eagerness to enjoy them for what they can provide. He will have a lot of suggestions to make about what to do. But mostly he will prefer there to be a kind of regularity and pattern to the visits; and he will appreciate a definite lead from the parent whom he does not see so much, and whose thinking and motivations may seem rather shadowy.

One reason for this better adjustment is that he has built up a feeling of how to treat each parent individually. The concept of "loyalty" to either side does not enter much into his thinking although attempts may of course be made to implant it, which may lead to guilt when he is enjoying himself with the "other" party. Loyalty, at this time, is often entirely relative to whichever parent he happens to be with. Each parent may be convinced that he feels happiest when he is with him or her. But it is natural for him to enjoy being with *both*.

But this does not often last through childhood. From ten to thirteen, a child of separated parents is liable to move on to another stage. Now he has a need to be more consistent, both in his feelings and in his dealings. He begins to be uncomfortable at the idea that he is having a good time with, or sharing the life of, the parent he does not support. The stronger the background of enmity in the marriage breakdown and in its aftermath, the more likely he is to become closely attached to one or other parent. This makes him emotionally less capable of developing his relationship with the other one. He may resolve the conflict he feels between his "loyalty" and the prospect of a happy visit by becoming a passive onlooker at these meetings rather than the active participant which he might have been in time past. His suggestions for what to do may dry up. He may forget arrangements. He may plead illness, which in some cases can be very real. Or he may simply refuse contact altogether—perhaps complaining that they "just do not get along." The greater the identification with either parent, the stronger is the need to re-enact a kind of "divorce" between himself and the other parent in his turn. This is in addition to becoming "loyal," and involves the child actually seeing himself as sharing in the personality and the life and fortunes of the parent with whom he identifies. Accordingly he re-enacts the divorce: now he is *really* on the side of the parent to whom he feels allegiance—why, he is actually *being* that parent, to some extent.

It should be stressed that although an eleven-year-old often develops this kind of "loyalty" to the parent with whom he is living, he does not *necessarily* opt for the custodial parent. Identification need not be with the parent of the same sex, although it may be more obvious when it is.

A complicating factor during this period is, of course, puberty. The majority of children nowadays will have experienced puberty by the time they are fourteen. Psychiatrists sometimes feel impelled to point out to anxious separated parents that the effects of puberty can make many a child feel and act rather strangely irrespective of their home life. This is a problem time for "normal" children in "normal" families. But it is also true that concentration is being focused—sometimes hurriedly and all at once—by the events of puberty on the sexual side of human beings, and on family life, which may cause a reappraisal of either or both parents. Children may not reappraise them in very flattering terms. Wondering whether the subject has to be skirted round in discussion with the absent parent can lead to visits becoming less natural and more forced in tone.

From fourteen years onwards, much of the personality and the interests of a young person are not only established, they are clear-cut. If he does not *like* either parent—if he does not appreciate that parent's company—this is by now very difficult to alter. He is no longer a child who can be won over, gradually, to a more sympathetic point of view. He can still be impressed by kindness, of course, or by discovering a new source of help or confidence, but there is a back-log of experience and attitude that shapes his thinking. You can find him interesting things to look at or do, and he will enjoy receiving gifts; but you will now only marginally influence a basic like or dislike.

It can be different if you have had no contact for some time, because then the teenager may have a more open mind. But now he "knows what he likes" and it is wisest to recognize this. Forcing companionship on him beyond what he seems to enjoy may be blowing in the wind. Better to have fewer, successful visits than frequent boring ones in which tempers get strained.

But like or dislike, one big advantage that a separated parent can offer a teenager is a willing ear. This is the opportunity to talk to someone who will be sympathetic, but far enough removed from day-to-day tension to provide some objectivity and perhaps a second opinion. This role of friendly adviser can be important, and very rewarding. In one sense it represents a graduation—to mutual help and understanding between adults.

4 : Making It Work

When a Saturday parent visits his children and takes them out for the day, a whole range of different things can happen. It's not all roses. Problems and unpleasantness can be there too. In this chapter I want to nail down some of the difficulties and suggest some ways of bypassing them or making them less infuriating or alarming.

In any event, I hope the point has been made clearly by now that *even when* a whole lot of problems spoil the day, the contact is almost always worth it. Whatever happens, there is no point in breaking the link or allowing it to decay.

TIMING

This is one of the most frequent causes of trouble. It is much easier to agree on the timing of a visit when both parents are fully in agreement that the visit is desirable. Arrangements are also much less agonizing to make if you live reasonably nearby. The other major factor is life-style: when people are very busy, and organize their lives down to the last quarter-hour, of course there are going to be timing problems.

It is easy to tell people to pick a date well in advance, offer an alternative, agree on something and stick to it. Human beings, however, are not on production lines. They fall ill, they have other obligations that take them by surprise, and the trains they board do not always run on time. Things can go wrong. If you show some allowance for human nature—on both sides of the wall—you will have less nail-biting and fewer arguments when the door in the middle of the wall opens and your child passes through.

Regularity is easier for some than for others. But younger children, particularly, find something very reassuring in regularity. It shows them that you care enough to fix on and preserve a time that is "theirs" and only partly yours. If a child knows that you are arriving about such-and-such a time every week, or every two weeks, he has a feeling that something good between him and his parent is continuing. If he cannot predict when the next meeting will be, this contact no longer seems solid or reliable. When possible, it makes sense to have a particular time agreed on for visiting so that, first, the children know about this, and gain in reassurance and confidence; and, second, fewer and less complicated arrangements are needed for agreeing on the details.

The big advantage in this second point is that you are not negotiating so often or reawakening the emotions that surround the whole idea of the visit. It could also be said in support of regularity that such a system makes it more difficult for anyone to make a mistake.

What is convenient for one person is unfortunately not the same for somebody else. You cannot expect, if you are coming from outside, to dictate precisely when and where the visit should happen. You have not the slightest idea what plans you may be disturbing. On the other hand, you have a right to some consideration from the other side too. Dictating times is an unreasonable idea, whoever is trying to impose his will. If both parties are thinking more about the children, they will try to work out some arrangement that is not too difficult for either of them. In other words, they will be grownup about it.

It follows from this that if it is necessary to change a visiting time for some reason, efforts should be made to let others know as far in advance as possible. Nobody likes to be told at the last minute that the visit is off for that weekend. It often means a whole chain-reaction of alternative arrangements.

It also follows that it's well worthwhile keeping lines of communication open, so that news about any timing changes can be transmitted as quickly as possible. Many take pains to cut themselves off as far as possible, only to regret it when information affecting their plans fails to come through in time for them to react. I mean, for example, people who change their telephone numbers and only tell their new friends about it; or those who instruct the switchboard operator at work never on any account to switch through or take messages from an ex-wife or an ex-husband.

Here are some other examples, taken directly from real life, which illustrate how people needlessly make trouble for others— and, eventually, for themselves too—where timing is concerned. Everybody suffers, not least the children, when any of these happens:

> She telephoned at lunch time (on Saturday) to say that she'd just arrived; she wanted to pick the children up at two. When I said that one of them had a swinning lesson at three, she told me that the children "will forget all about that as soon as they know their *mother's* here."

> Nobody knows when H is going to come to see the children. Of course he's very busy . . . but he just seems to want to leave it until he feels like it, or he suddenly finds he's got the spare time. When Jack asks if his daddy is going to be coming to see him again soon, I have to tell him I just don't know.

> My ex-wife is really most unreasonable. Always has been. The other weekend I'd forgotten all about the office golf tournament. There's a team event, and I was expected to do my bit. I suddenly realized it was the day I was due to see the children, the very morning—when somebody was already driving over to pick me up. I phoned right away, but I really got an earful over the phone, I can tell you.

Of course it's not all one-way. I've been given plenty of examples of last-minute cancellations, coming from the other side. A remarkably frequent one is the message stuck on the door saying something like "Sorry, tried to reach you but couldn't. Make it next week." But the point is that *none* of it helps, whoever is doing it. Children rapidly come to associate a visit with a hectic, troubled, unpredictable period that threatens to make anyone around them nervous or bitter.

PUNCTUALITY

Children do not need to be told when somebody is late. They can sense it in the air. It builds up the tension before a visit if you arrive some time after everyone was expecting you.

If you are regularly unpunctual, it conveys a message too. It tells a child that he is not important enough, in your eyes, to rate being met on time, and that you are a less reliable person than his other parent. In some cases it tells him that this is a relaxed, casual, adult way to treat close relations, which may be a style to admire and to cultivate.

Sometimes, when younger children are expecting their visit from a Saturday parent, they compete with each other to determine who can see him first. It's a great moment when first one then the other starts shouting towards a figure approaching from the distance, ''Here comes Daddy!'' The more regular and the more punctual the visits are, the more excitement and the less frustration. Apart from being a heart-warming scene, it proves something: it is evidence that the children are integrating the visits into their lives in a way they really enjoy.

Punctuality is important at both ends of the visit. If you say that you are bringing a child back at a certain time, that is a promise. Occasionally it proves very difficult to keep—in which case a telephone call explaining why and setting a new time limit is only common courtesy. It helps your cause too. If you have a record of making things easier for the other parent by sticking to a schedule, you are far more likely to succeed when asking for a special deal, for example a late evening visit to a movie or an overnight stay.

In some cases, children get very worried about time-keeping too. Some are told by one parent, ''Make sure he brings you back by six o'clock sharp.'' This is not very good practice when it is done with such vehemence as to unnerve the child to the point where he is always asking the time, and urging ''Shouldn't we be getting home now?'' But some children do this *spontaneously,* which is an important possibility to bear in mind. It usually indicates concern over loyalties—almost as if he is working it all out in terms of the time that is allowed for being ''disloyal,'' or enjoying life with the absent parent. No point in getting angered by this (although it is certainly irritating). It is part of the child's way of coming to terms with his conflicts and if it helps him to carve up visiting days into ''mother's'' and ''father's'' time, so be it.

One word of warning—a child's anxiety to return on time may

be expressed in the words, "Can't you drive *faster,* Daddy?" It takes a little self-control not to respond to this, and to drive safely.

When the children are older they will have their own arrangements for the evening after a visit. Lack of punctuality then may mean missing something that is important to them although it may mean nothing to you. If you unwittingly make them late for a judo match, or a meeting with a particular friend, they will be less eager to come out with you again.

PICK-UP AND RETURN

A social worker I interviewed gets asked by her husband every Saturday morning: "How many parcels are we expecting today?" It is hardly surprising that at certain times their house feels like a post office. Collections have to be made each Saturday, at fixed hours. If a child arrives late, either before a visit or after it, then she must find out if a plan has been changed and why. It is a service that the social worker offers less enthusiastically than she used to. For one thing, the demand has increased to the point where she has to keep a book with details about each child and about both halves of the family. She has to brief her husband if any trouble is expected. It has eaten into her social life and now it needs to be kept under control:

> If somebody said to me, "I can't stand the sight of him," I used to tell them, "Don't worry, you can bring the child here in the morning, I'll hand him over, and I'll give you a call when the child comes back." But I'm less generous with my time now. If a mother's afraid she's going to get beaten up, that's different. Of course I'll help then. Or if it's obvious the child just isn't going to see his father at all, unless I offer a pick-up point.

There are two other reasons, apart from fear of unmanageable numbers, why this social worker (and others like her) are discouraged from helping in this way. One is that the divorced parents sometimes start looking on it as part of the job. It is nothing of the sort: when anybody offers this—be it a social worker, a teacher, a clergyman, a relative or a friend of the family, each of whom has a chance of getting involved in being an intermediary—he does it because he is kind. It is not something to be taken for granted. The other reason for discouragement is the parents' attitudes when something goes wrong. If a child fails to turn up, or comes back late, or minus a sweater, there is no logical way in which the intermediary can be blamed. But blamed they are. When the emotion is running strong, more thoughtless parents (whether they are the ones living with their children or not) will lash out at the nearest available target. Nobody enjoys being a target if he or she does not have the responsibility for getting everything right in the first place.

This leads to the question of whether an intermediary is needed at all. There are extreme situations when this is probably the case. But it is too often an unnecessary imposition on other people. The motivation may often be to want to prolong a demonstration of the fact of the split to a third party.

Reference has already been made to the comparatively good relationships and adjustment, found in a research study, where children had the opportunity to use their bicycles freely between one home and the other. There are different ways of looking at this. One is to decide that easy, frequent access leads to less disturbance. Another is to suppose that a simplified approach is natural and less emotionally laden. But it also suggests there are benefits when the *child*, as well as each of the parents, has an opportunity to arrange, or join in arranging, contact. This implies that the formalities of a rendezvous at hours fixed by intermediaries, on neutral ground, may be counterproductive if they tend to protract hostility and stress. If the pick-up point at grandma's, or wherever, is the only way of keeping access going while avoiding hysteria, well and good. Otherwise, it is worth bearing in mind these points made by three different sets of parents:

Rick and Les

> **We** [i.e., absent parent and second wife] settled down within biking distance of the boys. What a change this made! They already had the idea [at ten and eight] that they could phone when they wanted to come over. But that meant planning, and they are not great planners. They go on impulse. With their bikes, they get this idea that they'll come over and spend the night. They ask their mom, and they're on the road. Sometimes they don't think about phoning, which makes it difficult. . . . But it's wonderful to see them just turning up.

They wave through the window and say, 'Dad, we've got our pyjamas!' Of course, it can work *both* ways. Sometimes they decide they want to go back to their mom early. Well—that's OK. They go under their own steam.

Lindsey

After a lot of trouble (including making arrangements to pick Lindsey up from people who just were not at home that afternoon, etc.), I suddenly hit on the right idea. I made it a rule that Lindsey would give me a telephone call every Tuesday evening after she gets home from school. Then we talk about the coming weekend, and what we are going to do. I tell her my car will be near the front of her house at such-and-such time. If she has something else to do that weekend, or if I'm going away on business, we discuss it, have a talk about things, and leave everything until the *next* Tuesday. She tells her mother what we decide. And of course her mother realized pretty quickly that she could let me know about any plans for trips that she was making that might conflict. It's a very simple system and the best thing about it is it's *direct*. I know what Lindsey wants, because it's coming from her.

Sometimes, at first, either Lindsey would forget or her mother tried to discourage the phone calls. I'm not sure which—I suspect a bit of both. (Lindsey was eight when the system began.) I taught her to reverse the charges, always, so there wouldn't be any financial excuse. I left it until about eight o'clock, and then telephoned with a lot of worry in my voice. "What's wrong with Lindsey? What's the matter? Why hasn't she phoned?" Her mother soon got in the habit of reminding Lindsey if she forgot.

My ex-wife and I still aren't on speaking terms. But we don't have to be. I see a lot of Lindsey (about every other weekend, for two or three days), and she talks much more easily now about the whole situation. If she worries, she doesn't show it. She enjoys herself at my place, and she's happy at home. . . . I wouldn't go back to writing letters, and meeting her at the corner, and all that gobbledegook.

Régine

The quotation from the third study requires a little explanation. Régine had been picked up by her father for a visit every other week between the ages of two years and three and a half years. Then her mother refused to allow further visiting on the grounds that the child "doesn't like it." Sensing that something of this kind might occur, as well as in order to compile an attractive album,

Régine's father's second wife had taken photographs at nearly every visit. The majority of them showed a very happy child. On legal advice, Régine's father sued for custody. The photo album was produced in evidence.

The judge adjourned everything, and took Régine, her mother and me into his back room. Then he tore a strip off us both.

He spoke sharply to her for discouraging Régine from wanting to see her father, and get on with him. The photos, he said, made it perfectly obvious that Régine enjoyed herself *if she was allowed*. Then he turned on me. "As long as you go on making a tense scene over every visit, then Régine will never enjoy it. When you collect Régine, what do you do?' I told him I called in at the lady's who runs the laundromat on the corner, and picked her up at two o'clock as we'd arranged. "That's pretty damn stupid for a start," he said. "Next Saturday—are you both free this Saturday? Yes?—you go to Régine's mother next Saturday instead." Turning to my ex-wife, he told her, "And you're going to make him a cup of tea." Then he looked me straight in the eye and said, "You're going to sit down and drink your cup of tea, like an adult human being. You're going to enjoy it and you're going to say 'thank you.' Ten minutes, and then you can go." We were all too surprised to say anything.

The old judge said Régine would get some strange ideas about how mature adults behave if we were at arm's length all the time, or dealing through third parties. I think he knew what he was talking about. We've had a few rows over money, but it's been plain sailing for the past four years as far as visiting goes. And if something happens—like once, when Régine fell over and banged her nose—I can talk straight to her mother, and we can all meet if need be. Régine stays for a few days sometimes. She has some food allergies, and if I'm doubtful about something I want to get her I can talk to her mother easily. The lady at the laundromat was very nice but she didn't know much about that.

Oh yes, and we never went back into court. The judge told us not to be so silly, and to pay off the lawyers right away, because we couldn't afford them.

There is an obvious connecting link in these three very different cases. Each of them is an example of success in maintaining contact coming from workable, direct communications, which become more natural and less taxing for the children. The same solution would probably *not* work in each case. The system used for

Régine, for example, is hard to imagine in the case of Lindsey or even for Rick and Les. Everybody has to find his own route. But, if that route makes more use of direct questions and answers in a practical, unemotional way, you are more likely to succeed: your child is not constantly reminded of powerful, half-understood feelings that prevent one parent ever seeing or talking to the other.

Not everyone can deal directly. Hence the need for people like the lady in the laundromat. Sometimes the emotional tide is running too strong, and you need an intermediary.

Very often relatives find themselves in this role. (Occasionally it is quite obvious that a relative has *selected* this role.) There is an advantage if the relative's house is near by, and is well known to the child. It helps if this pick-up can seem more like a natural extension of the family territory than a randomly chosen station on the Trans-Siberian Railway. The problem is when the relative, whoever it is, has already come out heavily on one side or another. An intermediary has to be someone whom *both* parents believe is objective, and unlikely to play political games. Social workers, clergymen and others who have long experience of presenting a sympathetic but not over-sympathetic face to both factions have the advantages of the right training for the job.

If you use an intermediary, do not abuse him or her. He *has* to stick to the rules when dealing with each parent. He has a right to his own time and privacy. It is also natural (as happens sometimes) that children suddenly find they like it very much at this person's house. It may seem to them a haven of freedom from emotional tension. Don't resent this: try instead to interpret what it means, because your child may be trying to say something important to both his parents—"Lay off!"

REFUSAL

It is a very chilling moment for a Saturday parent when he hears "I'm sorry, but Johnny simply doesn't want to see you."

What does it mean?

Sometimes it comes as a total surprise. One weekend Johnny is there, laughing, playing, joining in. The next weekend there is this strange about-turn.

The last chapter dealt with the main changes in attitude at different ages among children in split families. One of the most common changes leading to a sudden refusal to go out with the Saturday parent is a loyalty crisis at the age of about nine or ten years old. But there are other kinds of refusal at any age. If possible, you should try to determine which of these categories is concerned. Don't leap to conclusions—particularly over the first, since you probably only have partial information. Refusal could stem from one, or from a combination, of these reasons:

1 : discouragement by the other parent;
2 : something unpleasant about the way the visit is arranged;
3 : something unpleasant about the visit itself;
4 : holding out for treats, presents, etc.;
5 : boredom;
6 : preference for some other activity;
7 : being anxious not to miss out on contact with friends of the same age group—or a particular friend.

(Being ill, or overtired, may also cause refusal, but not prolonged refusal.) When a mother discourages a child from appearing for a visit, it may be an open attempt at severing the link. For example, she may say:

"It's not good for the children. I'm not going to allow it. And they don't want to see him/her anyway."

It may never be communicated, in point of fact. The parent may simply pack up and leave for a town two hundred miles away. Provided no national boundary is crossed, this is consistent with the requirements of a court order guaranteeing access to the parent who has not got custody, while effectively making access very difficult. Some suggestions for counteracting this are given in Chapter 9.

More commonly, access is refused by a mother *conditionally:* "You're behind on your payments. Pay up or you can't see them."

If you *can* make the payments, and you have actually lagged behind, there is not much you can complain about. If you cannot, you should appeal.

Another kind of discouragement is also fairly common:

My mom used to say to me when she helped me on with my coat and scarf, "Now you're leaving me all alone for the rest of the day.'' And she'd look like she was going to cry. One day I cried, and said I wasn't going to go out with daddy any more, I wanted to stay with my mom. There was a row on the doorstep, I remember, and I was told to get back upstairs. About a year later it was mostly forgotten, and I started going out with him again.

Finding out about it is another matter. Sometimes you can guess from the sort of answer you get to casual questions such as ''How's your mom? Is she well?'' or ''I suppose your mom's been looking forward to a little peace and quiet this afternoon, hasn't she?''

There are many occasions when a child loses his temper, throws a tantrum, or bursts into tears in the course of a visit. In a way, this is to be expected. Keep it in perspective: any normal child in any normal home is liable to act this way sometimes. If there is a highly charged emotional background to weekend visiting, such a scene may even be helpful by providing an emotional release. There is no point in feeling guilt or failure if this happens from time to time. But frequent or continual tears, sighs, sad looks, and refusal to enjoy visits have to be analyzed for what they mean, before they lead to outright refusal.

The answer can be simple or complex. One little girl of six used to love weekending with her father until it involved visits to his new wife's home. Here she developed fear and loathing of a cairn terrier, who barked whenever she appeared. Her father realized she disliked the dog, but hoped she would get used to it. But she suddenly refused to join up with her father again. Many a mother would have been tempted to regard this as evidence of rejection of the father's new wife. But in this case, the girl's mother paid attention to all the evidence—which included two nightmares about dogs. She offered her interpretation, suggesting that they should promise a dog-free environment. Once visiting was organized on neutral ground, it took place again happily, with no fuss. Eventually she was introduced to the dog again, out of doors, and the lead was offered to her. Nowadays she doesn't mind cairn terriers, and enjoys staying with her father and stepmother.

But this was an easy problem. When the parents have two very different attitudes towards discipline, it can be more unsettling and less easy to identify as a problem. Differences in tolerance of food preferences, choice of clothes to wear, noise level indoors and outdoors, treatment of furniture, and cleaning up after a mess—all these and many other factors may in total represent two lives, each with its own set of rules, to which a child has to adapt. It may not be easy. One child interviewed—who, at thirteen, had decided not to visit her father's home any more—complained that she'd been made to finish every scrap of food on her plate. Since she disliked the food served in his house, this regularly made her feel sick. Her mother supported this account independently, pointing out that the turn-ups of her daughter's jeans had always been filled with secreted food after every visit.

This is not an isolated case of divergent discipline. After all, many divorces have as one of their causes a feeling of being uncomfortable with the way the other partner wants to organize life at home. Naturally, this kind of difference gets reflected in the way children are treated. With few exceptions, children are not chameleons: they are not equipped to change their behavior from Friday to Saturday and resent having to do so.

Of course you have your own standards, and you have a right to point out what the rules are in your home. The question is how far you can reasonably expect a child to adapt. Remember that your child may not recall precisely what your rules are, and may want to discuss why you impose them, and whether they are really important.

If they discover that you are prepared to *pay* for the pleasure of their company, many a child will appreciate the opportunity for a quick profit. Holding out on visits unless there is a present or some money forthcoming is unpleasant but part of real life. It usually happens when an absent parent has been recklessly trying to buy love and friendship with gifts of various kinds. The closer they are in their interests and likes, the less this will happen between a parent and child. But as soon as a habit forms that is based on suggestions like "Why not come with me instead this weekend, and we'll go and have a look at some bicycles?," the bribe starts becoming more significant in the child's mind than the relationship itself. Anybody can become corrupted. And anybody can then play the same trick on the corruptor.

Another reason for refusals is particularly hard to accept. This is when a child becomes, quite simply, *bored*. Nobody likes to admit that they may be boring. But nearly all parents bore their children sometimes. Bear in mind that, whereas a young child definitely enjoys an element of predictability in periodic visits, which tells him that there *is* a pattern in your priorities that includes him, this can change rapidly once the age of about eleven is reached. Then, if they feel more secure, they naturally want to live life to the full. "Oh no! Not lunch with grandma *again!*" Don't give in each time, but observe whether the protests, particularly the silent protests, seem to be building up. It's a warning that if you do not vary the diet you may soon meet a blunt refusal to come out with you.

At one extreme, perhaps, is Michael, who at thirteen was expected to wait at the corner of the street for his sister-in-law to drive by and drop him off at his father's place. Michael's father worked nights, so that early on Saturday afternoon he might still be in bed. There was a strict rule that no noise should be made to disturb his sleep. This meant no radio, and no friends around. Television was all right, provided the sound was off. But the only place to sit down comfortably was in the minute kitchen. To supplement his income, his father repaired television sets, and parts were literally everywhere. It was absolutely forbidden to touch any of these things in case some vital piece became lost. The apartment was on the fifth floor, and there was no garden below.

What followed was almost invariable, summer and winter.

When his father woke up, it was to have breakfast, and to choose "a good horse" for the afternoon's races. There was usually a TV set to finish repairing and to deliver. Then a walk to the corner store where a man accepted bets on horses. Sometimes there was a brief celebration after a race with an ice cream or a chocolate bar. Sometimes not. When they got back home it was usually time for Michael to be picked up by his sister-in-law.

Michael's father can only be criticized up to a point. He was always in debt, however hard he worked to escape it. Materially he had little to offer. But he had no understanding that sheer boredom made Michael want to spend his Saturday afternoons elsewhere, with his friends. His father maintains that Michael's mother's friends had been getting at him, and that they had made him despise his father for being poor. But the way Michael describes it gives the impression that while he has a lot of affection for his father he feels he was made to suffer long enough in a kind of voluntary imprisonment. "If Mom and Dad hadn't been divorced, and we'd all been living together, I wouldn't have had to spend that time with him then, would I?" This thought had occurred to him when talking to his friends at school. When he was old enough, he decided for himself what the visiting should be. After a rift of a couple of months he went back to see his father again—but on his own terms. He uses his bicycle, he brings a friend over; if his father isn't up, he goes off for an hour or so and comes back.

This is probably an extreme case. But it makes you see what really repetitive visits are like through a child's eyes. And note the logical point Michael makes about how he would have avoided all this in a "normal" family. Partially avoided, at any rate. Access to the other parent is supposed to *help* these children, not drive them up the wall.

There is a real problem when younger and older children are involved at the same time. If they are at different stages of development, it makes more sense to suit both sides by having a regular arrangement for a younger child and a variable one for an older child. Occasionally you will see them both. But, while every Sunday may mean a rendezvous with the younger one, both you *and* the older child will have separate ideas for meeting. You need to discuss these ideas and sort them out. This is how growing up is meant to happen. You cannot compress a young, active, intelligent person in a jelly mold.

When you establish a pattern of weekending, as opposed to daytime visits, you have a much better chance of satisfying the needs of all age groups. This depends, however, on your being prepared to do two things. First, to refuse to allow one child to dominate your attention; second, to be relaxed about the comings and goings of an older child—within the bounds of their sense of responsibility—and about visits by his or her friends.

This section on boredom is incomplete without reference to activities (see Chapters 5 and 6).

But note that your child may think that he or she has a better idea for passing the time. Anybody who wants to excel at something, whether it is music, disco dancing or running, is going to get fanatical about it at some stage. The studious may need to spend more time on homework, too.

Don't fight against this kind of counter-attraction: *join it*.

This does not mean going to the same disco scene (although it *might* mean going along to watch or take part in football, skating, or any number of things). The more you show you can compromise on timing to help your children participate in what they really enjoy, the more they will associate you with that enjoyment. They will talk to you about it, and you will keep mutual contact, despite losing some physical closeness.

The same applies to friends. Your child's friends should be yours too, if at all possible. You won't like the look of them all (parents never do), but your child cannot be just an individual to you. As they grow older, children increasingly become parts of society. If they know that you know this, they will find time for you.

HEALTH AND MONEY

I have left these two obvious problem areas until the last. In some cases, they are the most difficult to deal with.

If you do not have the physical ability to deal with young children and prevent them from coming to harm in your house, there is no need to say goodbye for ever. There are plenty of cases where people from the local health and welfare office have arranged for "sitters" to help a disabled Saturday parent. Unless you are totally immobilized, this is usually more easily arranged at the house of someone (often a foster parent, but there are a number of volunteers) who is prepared to keep a watchful eye on your children during a visit. If you ask persistently, someone in local government will help you and put you in touch with either a social worker or a volunteer family, which will usually have children of similar age.

When you are immobilized, or in hospital, the clergy often come into the picture. Hospital visiting is often part of their routine and some have been known to bring children of divorced parents with them. Social workers, and of course relatives, can help too, but it is hard to get a regular routine going, since all these people have other claims on their time.

Obviously you cannot expect to receive visits from children if there is any fear that your illness may be infectious, or if you are in a ward where infection may be transmitted by others.

Money naturally fits in here. If you are sick, but wealthy, you can arrange most things. If you are sick and poor, it is much more difficult.

Financial problems multiply as soon as one or the other half of the former marriage decides to move to another town. It is only reasonable to ask for a longer time in which to see your child if you have to spend a lot of time and money to reach him. Court orders have been varied to allow for this, where the parent living with the child has insisted on sticking to the letter of the law. Planning, preparing and saving up can make the visit more exciting when it is one visit instead of several. But making sure that the timing is properly understood by all is critical.

Less dramatically, there is the point that having little money reduces the number of exciting things that you can do with your children, *wherever* you are actually living. When you find yourself having to refuse a lot of your children's ideas, tell them straight: ''I can't afford it.'' They respect this more than if you are just evasive. But once you decide to spend more than usual on a present or a treat, don't spoil it for them: don't remind them how many hours of scrimping and saving it took. You gave it because you wanted to give it. That way they will be able to enjoy it, and not feel guilty about it.

There are *always* things to do with children, no matter how little money you have. Some are suggested in the following chapter.

5 : Shorter Visits

The last chapter set the scene, so to speak, for a visit to your child. It discussed the problems that can get in the way of arranging a visit at all, or of enjoying it in a reasonably positive atmosphere. It's now time to consider what you are actually going to *do*. Meeting is one thing. But human beings want more than mere getting together.

For a child up to the age of ten, try to get some element of *ritual* into the visit. Note the difference between the ways a six-year-old and a twelve-year-old will comment "We always go down this street to the station, don't we?" The younger child will be smiling, as likely as not. He is discovering a pattern, however unimportant a detail it may seem, in his relationship. The older child, nearly in his teens, may choose the same words to express a pained resignation that means "We're doing the same things, over and over again."

In fact, both want some variety in short-term visits. Simply going to another apartment or house, even if there's a garden outside, and alternating between kicking a football and watching television, becomes pretty boring after a while. It may mean careful planning and timing, even more careful budgeting, and keeping an alternative program up your sleeve in case of bad weather, but thinking up interesting changes and surprises is part of the essence of being an interesting person, of finding out where your children's interests and talents really lie, and building an inexhaustible store of points of contact and conversation. This is what you really *want*, isn't it?

It needs work, and thought, for these reasons:

1 : Younger children need an element of ritual, as mentioned above.

2 : They are often resistant (at *first*) to an idea that represents change, that they haven't thought about.

3 : They may have fantasized another, old favorite activity with you for that very day.

4 : Sometimes you will be *bound* to make a bad choice—which may prejudice some children against "experimenting" again.

5 : What may be ideal for a younger child may not go down well with an older one.

You need to be very firm, sometimes, with young television addicts, in your endeavor to vary the diet. If you give way, you may be cooping up another child who is not as interested in the same program. State firmly your decision at the beginning of the visit. Try a compromise, perhaps, such as "No. This afternoon we're going to a streetcar exhibition. If we get back by four, you can watch the second half of the game."

Then, be prepared for the disbelieving sneer—"Streetcars?! Oh *no!*" Don't argue. Just cough, and say "Oh yes."

Incidentally, heading for the television set and watching for an hour or so is an interesting symptom in itself. If it suddenly becomes a regular habit, as opposed to something sparked off by a particular show, it is often a sign that your child is opting out of what he regards as an emotional tangle. It can be a way of showing you that he feels threatened by a crisis of loyalty if he gets too close to you or enjoys the time spent with you too much. When he goes back home he can truthfully report, "Oh, we didn't do much. We just sat around and watched TV." Don't give in. Compromise on certain programs, but set your rules and *stick to them.*

If other things are equal, then, there will be something (small or large, it doesn't matter) that you will do in the *same way* each visit; there will be something *new* that you will offer (whether it's a complete change or a variation), and you will aim at including something *active,* that you do together, and in which you interact.

Every now and then, something really important to your child will make him ask to spend the time in a way that cuts across your best-laid plans. Judge these things as they come up. Compromises have to be made, occasionally. If you *know* what is important to your son or daughter, you will anticipate these choices more easily. You will also be well advised to show some genuine interest from your side, in whatever is fascinating them. It may be a sport, a local fair, a particular film, a particular friend, or using a new skateboard or a bicycle. You may be able to join in, or you may not. But find out about it; ask questions (*remembering* what you were told last time).

Yet for the most part, the initiative for planning the day rests with you.

SHOW THEM WHERE YOU LIVE, IF YOU CAN

Sometimes an absent parent is ashamed of showing where and how he is living. This is a pity, because it is part of how you are living now. Your children are often very anxious to know what sort of house or apartment you have, and how you have arranged the objects, clothes and possessions that they associate with you. Your territory is part of you. They may not ask many questions about this, but they will usually jump at an opportunity to satisfy their curiosity.

This doesn't mean, obviously, that you should take your child home every time you meet. But it's good to have a point of reference. If you can give a telephone number, too, and instructions on how to call you by reversing the charges, that number *means a lot more* if it is connected with a place that has been seen, smelt and touched. A number is just a number in a child's mind. Telephoning Mommy or Daddy at home has meaning. It is much more likely to be done when a child wants contact. To a child's mind, it seems much more realistic that way.

There are other problems about bringing a child home. One is distance—which may necessitate a weekend stay. The other is the point that there may be somebody there whom you would prefer your child *not* to see, or whom the other parent has forbidden the child to see. The whole question of new friends and step-parents deserves a chapter to itself. But here it could be noted that whoever is there is part of your choice of how to live. And, even if an introduction seems too big a step to take, you can always choose a time when you will be alone there with your child.

It may seem a strange place to a young person's eyes. Make it more obviously a part of your life and a part of your child's life. Point out the objects that may be remembered as being yours. And try, if you can, to organize it so that there is a small section that belongs to, or is supervised by, your child. This could be just the corner of a mantelpiece or of a chest of drawers. Ask for advice at first, for instance: "I've got this picture of you, in a frame. Where do you think it will look best?" And be prepared to follow the suggestions made. Choice of an ornament—preferably something your child made at school some time ago—and choice of plants or flowers can follow. After that, it depends on what you judge your child's interests will dictate. One Saturday parent I know had to find a home in his bed-sitting-room for a collection of moths and larvae, which his ex-wife had ordered out of her house. It was always going to get sorted out, in trays with paper labels. This has never happened, although several starts have been made. His son still (at fifteen) checks up to make sure it is there, in a box in a cupboard under the stairs. It is a repulsive old box—from one point of view. It is dedicated territory from another. This is how links are made stronger.

Another Saturday parent was luckier. His daughter looked around critically on her second or third visit to the room he was renting. She had a strong sense of how a house should be run, even at the age of twelve. (Very possibly, she had been frustrated in working out her own plans at her own home, where her mother naturally believed in maintaining control.)

"First of all," she announced one rainy afternoon, "we're going to have to move the furniture around a bit. . . . Then I really think you could do with a change of wallpaper."

The idea of changing and improving her father's style of living really took hold of her imagination. For about half a year they used to work together at weekends. They did not always agree, but he admits that she had far better ideas than he had—even if they were sometimes expensive. What she was doing, in fact, was to take over, or rather resume, an active part in his life. Eventually she seemed to lose interest in that. But they established many points of contact, and still see each other often.

Your children cannot *own* you any more. But they can still own symbolic pieces of you. You want access to *them:* give them some access *to your home,* and they can lay claim to little parts of your life, as well as getting to know you better.

DO SOMETHING ACTIVE TOGETHER

Television is said, quite rightly, to disrupt communication in ordinary family life. Think how much more disruptive it can be when parent and child have only a few hours together every other week. I'm choosing television as a prime target because watching it is a passive activity *par excellence,* and because most children go through a stage of being compulsive viewers at some time of their lives. You could say they are lucky if it is only a stage.

Neither television, nor spectator sports, nor movies, nor theater, concerts and the like should be the subject of a ban. Banning them only makes them more desirable, during access visits as well as in ordinary life. But they should certainly be controlled.

If you do something active with your child, you are participating in something. You have to talk to each other, smile, shout, encourage or discourage, depending on how it is going. You could be out on a country ramble, playing football, chasing each other round a playground, admiring dinosaurs at the museum, or monkeys at the zoo. You could be taking a lesson together in archery, pottery, drawing, judo, trampoline, archaeology or whatever is your fancy. You could be tying on your flies and casting into a stream. Or you could be having a talk—about why quadratic equations are tricky, how certain machines work, or why it is that somebody, a teacher perhaps, is so difficult to understand and satisfy.

All this is being active. If you can just do two or three of these things together, or anything like them, you will be getting a lot out of each visit. More, certainly, than the exchange of a few words during a commercial break.

MAKE SURE THEY ENJOY IT

Nothing could be worse than to insist on an activity—however active—week after week, if your child is starting to loathe it. Here are some hints for maximizing the chances that you are *both* going to enjoy yourselves.

Find out first what kinds of things interest your children. Do they tend to be more studious, or more athletic, or are they practical and interested in crafts? Which studies? Which sports? Which crafts? If you've been away for some time and there hasn't been much contact, you may have to rely on memory or chance remarks. That's the positive side. You should also make a few notes on what they *dislike*. They may hate sports, hate anything that has anything conceivably educational about it, or hate the feeling of helplessness when they tackle anything practical.

Now work out a series of possible things that you can do together, trying to aim more towards what your child likes, and away from what on past experience is liable to prove unpopular. I say "series," because you may well miss the mark the first time, and you should be prepared for some trial and error. Furthermore, you should have in mind what to try the next time, even if you are successful with the first planned activity.

Aim to change to something else *before* your child has already had enough. Stopping something before people are tired of it is usually a guarantee that they will look back on the experience with pleasure. If you get a loud demand, such as *"Please* can't we go back there next time?" you must use your judgment. If it's going really well, why spoil the fun? But you could suggest trying something else, and *then* deciding.

Don't expect everything to fall into place if you simply arrive at the scene and hope that everything will work out.

"I blame myself for putting them off fishing," one parent reports. "I got these rods for myself and my two boys. We went to a reservoir where anybody's allowed to fish, and it was a complete disaster. I'd imagined that setting up hooks and floats and bait would be easy, because so many children do it without thinking. But it took a long time just finding out how to make it all work, and we kept getting entangled in trees, reeds, and one another's clothing. Everybody got impatient, and tempers were lost, mine included. Needless to say we caught nothing. And the weather turned very cold."

This is not being said against fishing. The same situation can arise with kites, model airplanes, or any activity where you need to get used to the equipment and to the situation. It's just a case history that tells against a *failure to plan*.

If this father had taken the trouble, one evening, to see how the fishing tackle was supposed to work, if he had gone down to the reservoir and noted the easy positions from which to fish, if he had observed what the other fishing folk were wearing by way of protective clothing, then he could have reduced the chances of a disaster.

He could also have worked out a fail-safe scheme, to keep in the corner of his mind. Some children are less patient than others and, even if everything had been superbly well organized, they might have become more and more fidgety as time went on and the fish refused to bite as rapidly as was desired. Then the alternative could have been presented—*before* mutiny broke out. Possibly they might have taken a football into a field near by. Or had a change of scene—turning the fishing expedition into a hike, or moving off to a recreation ground. Something to provide a change of pace, and to abort any sense of frustration.

These "secondary plans" are best chosen as *opposites* to the original, basic plan in terms of energy expenditure. If a child is fishing, visiting a museum, making a model, watching a puppet show—in sort, doing something quietly—then a welcome change of pace means doing something energetic and noisy. Vary the diet if you can. And if you are hoping for a few hours at a hobby, like fishing, and it doesn't work out as planned, switch them on to another activity where they can run, jump, shout, and, if they seem to need to, fight.

If something doesn't work, don't try to force it down. *Wait* for a month or so, and try to approach it from a different angle. This deserves another word from the frustrated fisherman, quoted above.

> It might not have been so bad if I'd just left it at that. But I found myself looking at this tackle, in which I'd invested quite a few dollars, and two weeks later I thought we ought to try again. As soon as the boys saw the rods in the car, their faces turned sour. One tried saying, "Mom won't let us go fishing any more, she says it gave us bad colds." I got around this one by noting that they'd brought their parkas, and that if she'd been really worried she'd have told *me*. So they did a passive resistance number on me. They didn't talk. They gave one-word answers. They were

determined to hate every minute of it. Now I'd done a bit of practice with the rods in the mean time, but I hadn't bargained for a high wind; that reduced the whole fishing business to nonsense again. The kids obeyed orders, picked up their rods, and went through the motions. Suddenly I said, "Let's give it all up, we'll buy some chips and some coke, and we'll go to a friend I know who's got a dartboard. Have you ever played darts?" You should have seen their faces. It was like prisoners on parole. Just as well I did that, because I think they'd have stopped coming out.

Alternatively, he could have waited a month or so, and brought along somebody who really *did* know about fishing. He should have chosen a different spot to fish. He should have given the boys some books or articles about fishing in the mean time. If he had brought them in on choosing the right tackle, finding the right bait, and so on, they would have felt more involved. Hindsight is easy, of course.

In fishing, as in *any* active hobby which you want to develop to share as a pleasure with your children, you have to be prepared to lead them up to a point where *they* get enthused, and *they* start calling the tune, for example by suggesting and discussing where to go, when to do it, what equipment is needed next, what tips are good ones and which are old wives' tales. When you get this, you are in effect practically losing control. But then you are sharing something—and basically that is what you want.

LEAVE SPACE FOR TALKING TIME

Sometimes children need to talk more than at other times. It may be more obvious to you, if you observe them, than it is to them. They don't always know.

It's a shame to gear a whole visit to a fast-action, split-second, totally hectic program, if it means that any opportunity for quiet conversation is lost. This is not, unfortunately, something that you can tackle head on. Asking your child "Is there anything you particularly want to talk about?" is sure to drive it underground, but the want is still there. They may not be used to confiding in you. They cannot be sure you will help them.

There are ways round this, although you have to use your judgment as to which one works best. And, having found one, you cannot rely on it every time to turn the lock and open the door on what your child wants to know. As he grows, and as you both gain in the habit of communicating closely with each other, you need to develop more mature and more natural approaches.

Here are some methods which work well with younger children, up to the age of about ten, depending on how old they are emotionally as much as physically.

1 : Do something one-to-one with your child that is engrossing but repetitive. Cat's cradle is a perfect example. Pen-and-paper drawing puzzles, where you each contribute part of a more and more complicated picture, are another. This establishes contact between you, *even before* you start talking seriously. It lowers defenses against letting out questions or comments that may be a bit painful to bring to the surface. One Saturday parent claimed that with his son the best conversations (in the sense of the deepest, and in the end the most beneficial ones) always came when they were playing chess, for example: "If I move my knight there—that'll be a problem for you, won't it, Dad? Your—ahem—your queen, Dad, is under fire. . . . Do you talk to Mom ever, when I'm not around?"

2 : Put it into the third person. Another Saturday parent asks his four young children for important news via the family cat: "What's Toby been saying this week as he's prowled round the house?" When the answers are straightforward, such as "He says 'Miaow, I want my supper! I want my milk,' " or funny—"He says, 'Down with dogs,' " then there's not usually a great deal to talk about. When the answers are less positive, such as "Miaow, why are people shouting so much? I just want to go to sleep," they need rather careful probing. This particular answer led to a discussion about fights between brother and sister, of which they were both rather regretful and afraid, and tantrums with their mother, which made them even more afraid. Talking it through helped.

Many children would scorn make-believe conversations with cats (or dogs or hamsters, or teddy bears, whose words and "actions" are often the road towards finding out what is on your child's mind). More serious children will sometimes tell you what they think Grandma must be thinking when she visits. *Part* of the time it will be objective. *Part* of the time she will be the mouthpiece for personal problems.

3 : Put your child "in charge." The idea of being "king for a day" is usually fascinating for most children. Someone who says absolutely nothing about life at school may suddenly light up if asked, "Suppose you were the principal at your school, and you could do absolutely everything you wanted—what would you do?" Here again, if the talk is about nothing more than "ice cream all day long," "football every afternoon," and "teachers would be made to eat up all their cabbage and potatoes," the signs are good. But any desire to hurt other children, or a particular teacher, or to expel them, or to get out of the place completely, is worth further questions: "Did you just choose Mr. Williams by accident, or do you feel he's the best teacher to be locked in the basement?" The problem with the unpopular Williams will gradually work its way out.

4 : Ask for a drawing, or perhaps hold a drawing competition. The way in which the house or the members of a family are drawn can sometimes tell you whether something is the matter or not. Asking why someone has been drawn with such large hands may lead to a discussion of that person's strength or power, which may be frightening. But do not confuse artistic achievement with the purpose of the exercise—which is just to encourage talking. Don't let your child suspect, if asked the questions above, that you are criticizing the way he or she is drawing.

The following apply to any age:

5 : Prime conversation time is often just after strenuous activity, or something that demands a lot of effort and concentration, such as singing. For example: "I could never get through to Eric until we'd covered at least ten lengths of the pool, and we were hanging on the side, panting." Children talk more easily after jogging, too, or when resting, near the end of a long country walk. Singing a lot of songs, the noisier and rowdier the better, has a similar effect.

6 : Remember what you talked about last time. If you have to be reminded several times who a particular teacher is, and why he is to be loathed, then you are not proving to be a particularly good person in whom to confide.

7 : Don't over-promise. Listening sympathetically is one thing. Choosing what to believe and where to pitch in and help are different tasks. Sometimes a whole horror story about trouble at school is poured out for the sake of pouring it out. It is, if you like, a demand for attention and details are exaggerated purposely.

But avoid the Saturday parent's trap of promising to rush in like an avenging angel and change everything. You may need to do so once, in a serious crisis. Be absolutely certain of why you should intervene and what you are likely to achieve. You may not be able to help very much at school or at home. If your child's case seems worth pleading, by all means plead, preferably avoiding the accusation of over-reacting. But avoid promises. Meanwhile, listen, discuss, and say you will try to help. Discuss together what you might do. Knowing that you are on his side is usually more important than feeling that a change is going to be made.

PROVIDE SOMETHING FOR EACH CHILD

One of your children may be thirteen, the other five. You may be told you have to take both out on the same day "because that is the only convenient arrangement." First of all, question this. A thirteen-year-old is very unlikely to enjoy the same kind of outing as a five-year-old. Does "convenience" really matter so much that one or other of the children has to get bored?

Be prepared to compromise. Sometimes take out both. Sometimes the elder, sometimes the younger, just by themselves. Normal families work by compromise. Point this out, if you need to do so.

Next, remember that a thirteen-year-old has more commitments but more flexibility. He (or she) can help discuss and fix his own timetable with you, provided everybody is told in advance what this is going to be.

Short visits with children of mixed ages sometimes work, but can be frustrating. Where you find yourself having to take over both children or neither, insist on a long weekend instead sometimes. This will give the opportunity for each of them to have particular times with you, and you can plan so that each of them can do some of the things he or she likes.

Let's assume that you have both children for the same afternoon one Saturday—a thirteen-year-old and a five-year-old. With patience and ingenuity you can still make this work reasonably well.

For a start, get the older child on your side. Ask if he can help you with the younger one. (We'll make them brother and sister, respectively.) Discuss with the brother what kinds of toys and games the little one prefers nowadays, what she likes to eat and drink, and what warning signs there may be if she is going to lose her temper. Ask his advice, and listen to what he says. Let him understand that you need to tackle this problem as a team, and he will feel complimented. He may or may not have any practical suggestions. But he will be motivated to help you. Any jealousy he may feel towards her will also be bypassed (perhaps not completely) by the sense that you have put him on a different, more senior level.

Next, pick up your little girl and give her a cuddle. Don't force it: but the chances are that this is what she wants. If you don't show your affection for her in this way *early* in the afternoon, she will be hunting for it, possibly getting more frustrated and more tearful, as the day wears on. She may want to wrestle with you a bit. Fine. If she needs to act out some aggression towards you, again it is better to let this come quickly and easily. Encourage her elder brother to join in any embrace or rough-housing. Make him feel he belongs there too. But be prepared for some embarrassment and hesitation on his part: at thirteen you were like that, and you wanted something rather more subtle.

If you can get out of doors and stay there, so much the better. Recreation grounds are excellent for mixed age groups. The chances are that one will find a friend or some other children to play near to and show off to, while you can entertain the other one if he or she needs it. Or one can try out the swings and seesaws, while you exchange football passes with the other. The main thing to watch out for is faulty equipment (of which there is plenty), and you must be prepared for rapid rescue if anything too ambitious is attempted on the more challenging metal structures.

When there is a sign of boredom, take them off for a walk—but not too far, unless you are prepared to carry your little girl at least part of the way.

If you are out of doors and your boy wants to play with something special—such as a kite or a model airplane or whatever— that's fine. But either provide your younger child with something engrossing that will distract her or take over the task of entertaining her yourself. Above all, prevent her from sabotaging the special equipment that your son is fascinated by: he will hold *both* of you responsible if there is any trouble. Spare a moment or two for showing interest, asking intelligent questions and giving friendly advice, where your son's activity is concerned. But here it is more a question of setting and maintaining a scene where he can pursue it and take some pride in the fact that you are watching and perhaps learning a bit from him.

Your little girl may be quiet or she may be hyperactive or anything in between. If she tends towards shifting quickly from one thing to another, you have to pay her in her own coin. You cannot *stop* her from being easily distracted, nor can you stifle her need to run around, jump up and down, and risk her own safety every other minute. You need to be fit, and to be prepared to be a little childlike, if you are to survive this afternoon happily. Break into little games of tag—always letting her catch you after a struggle. Tell her you are an island at sea, and let her dance on your chest. Throw your coat on the ground and tell her this is a ship—while she is on it, she is safe. She may respond to fantasy games of this kind for a minute, or for half an hour—but she won't get bored. The more inventive you are, incidentally, the more your son will be tempted to come over from where he's been playing football, watch you, comment, and then pitch in with his own ideas.

Avoid outdoor programs which put too great a strain on the physical endurance or the patience of your younger child. Your boy may want to go for a long bike ride with you. Fix that up for another time. Even equipped with crash-helmet, windbreaker and gloves, your girl will rapidly be bored out of her mind, and may well catch cold. But fairs and other events with lots of different attractions— zoos, parks, open-air exhibitions of traction engines, even—can stimulate all three of you.

The chances are, of course, that it will rain. Don't just make it a shopping expedition. If you do, keep it brief. As discussed in an earlier chapter, your children are more interested in the act of your bringing something for them than the toy or dress or whatever it is they maintain they cannot live without. With your two children of five and thirteen in tow, you have a competitive situation. Each is interested in different things, but each (even the older one) will be anxious not to miss out on what the other is being given. Neither is particularly interested in the sections of a toy or sports shop that fascinate the other. Altogether, the sooner you get away from the shops the better for everybody's temper, and the less the frustration.

You will have to do some shopping with them sometimes, even if it is only for a chocolate bar or some fruit. Make it easier on yourself this way:

1 : Ask the older child's advice on what to get for the younger one, and turn it into a joint expedition in which he has an interest.

2 : Don't ask a young child (less than ten) to choose between objects. She will prolong the process, change her mind, infuriate her brother and the store clerk. . . . It may seem hard, but make it your choice, with a quick check such as "Do you *like* licorice, Tammy? Good. Here you are, then."

3 : If you are giving them pocket money, or if they want to be spending *their* money, that is different. They have a right to choose. But wait for them *outside* the shop, or away from the counter. You will find they make their transactions much more quickly.

4 : Ask your older child quickly what he wants. If you can't afford it, tell him—just like that. If he has a clear idea, and it is within your budget, give him a wink, and then whisper to the younger child, "Will you help me get something for Mike?" Again, you are sharing the expedition and avoiding making anyone bored. But you have to do it rather subtly when there is a thirteen-year-old at the receiving end. Hence the preparatory wink.

But shops are a substitute for doing something active. I class them with television. Always keep a list of real activities handy, to which you can add from time to time during the week, whenever an idea strikes you. You want four columns, headed like this:

Activity	Timing	Mike (13)	Tammy (5)
Science Museum	Mon.–Sat. 10:00–6:00 Sun. 2:30–6:00	YES	Yes?
Zoo	Summer 9:00–6:00 Winter 10:00–5:00 (every day except Christmas Day)	YES	YES
Doll's Exhibition	Weekends 1:00–6:00	No?	YES
Children's Drama Classes	Sats 10:00–12:00	Yes?	Yes?

Leave a space for other similar away-from-home activities.

Under each 'activity' item, it helps to write down how to get there and the length of the journey time.

The list goes on with a second part, which is devoted to activities you can organize at home, or in a friend's house, on wet days. (Sometimes the enthusiasm will be such that you will have to include them on fine days, too.)

Activity	Tolerance limit	Mike (13)	Tammy (5)
Building a doll's house	1 hour tolerance	Yes	YES
Scrapbooks	½ hour tolerance	YES	Yes
Snap, etc.	½ hour	Yes	YES
Stamp collection	½–1 hour	YES	No
Painting etc.	½–1 hour	Yes	YES

The size of the "Yes" or "No" varies according to liking for the activity, *or* the degree to which it will be acceptable as a way of helping Dad (or Mom) and keeping a little sister quiet.

Depending on the space you have available (and the amiability of neighbors) you can add more energetic, noisier activities on the list. One Saturday parent offers handball, shuffleboard, wrestling, and a kind of archery (not all at the same time) in a large room for which he has no other important purpose. Several of the local children join up to play at whatever is going on there on rainy days at the weekend. The more successful you are, the more you find yourself liable to become a junior community center.

On a short visit day, then, when you observe in the morning that the sky is a gray helmet, and the weather forecasts talk of storm and flood, look at your list. Decide which is best: to spend part of the time at an official, organized activity, and part of the time at home, or to devote all the time to one or the other. With your two children of different ages, you would be well advised most times to try to split the time, making sure that something of particular interest to *each* child is included. Timing, and money, may not always make this possible.

Choose, then, a visit from the first half of the list and two or three items from the second half. Have one or two alternatives in mind, in case one child suddenly rebels totally against something you thought they liked. Always try to keep the list topped up with new additions. And asterisk anything that works really well.

Some Saturday parents are often stumped by the problem of what to do that's new, especially at home. But there are ideas everywhere. A look through the list of courses offered at night school is an easy source of inspiration. You don't even have to sign up for a course. The idea is the thing—whether it be modelling, learning about engines, making puppet theaters, making home-make jewelry. . . . You then need to find out how to start off in a modest way, and how to switch into a higher gear if you all decide you like it.

Time and money are always going to be constraints. But often the most satisfying pursuits for your children, both the older *and* the younger this time, are those which can be turned on and off almost without thinking, and with a minimum of equipment. Your five-year-old Tammy will almost certainly most relish that moment when you go down on all fours and become a wolf (friendly, mind—not too fierce) and when you invite her to ride on your back. Mike will want to know just how far away he is from bending your arm back during an Indian wrestling match. Both will want to run races with you. Both will want to play their own version of football with you. Have you tried passing a football back and forth at speed with a thirteen-year-old, while carrying a five-year-old on your shoulders? If you have, the chances are you make a good Saturday parent.

Finally, just to make sure that none of those little things that can be so demoralizing on short visit days goes wrong, consult this checklist until you have committed it to memory:

1 : Know when and where you are going to stop for something to eat and drink.

2 : Encourage a visit to the washroom just before departure.

3 : (Depending on age) observe and ask at regular intervals if anyone needs to use the washroom. But never ask this question if no washroom is visible—the power of suggestion is considerable.

4 : Count clothing, parcels, toys, or whatever detachable items your children may have just prior to departure, and then at intervals.

5 : Know what you are going to do in case of

        cuts and grazes,

        nosebleed,

        diarrhea,

        anything needing medical supervision,

        car breakdown,

        finding nobody there at the return pick-up point,

before you actually need to do it.

6 : Any time your child goes out of your sight, for whatever reasons, agree first of all on a clear landmark where you will meet again.

7 : Rehearse the names of your children's main friends, so that you ask and answer questions about them intelligently.

8 : Just before leaving, at the end, ask if there are any messages that they were supposed to pass on to you.

9 : Just before leaving, ask yourself if there are any clothes, keys or information that *you* need to pass across.

10 : Always carry a box of tissues.

6 : Longer Visits

Some of the best times that Jim, now twenty, can remember in his childhood were when he was ten, and his brother and sister were thirteen and twelve respectively. He recalls visits that the three of them used to make to his father, who had left the family home some four years previously.

His father's apartment consisted of two rooms, a hallway, and a kitchenette. Every second weekend, for several months, one of these rooms became a dormitory, with three males on the floor in sleeping bags and the sister lording it by herself in the bedroom.

> I don't know why it should have been fun. Mad, really. Dad had no business taking us in like that. He asked us not to say too much about how we were packed in like sardines. I expect Mom knew more or less what was going on anyway. But we had a terrific time. It was all so different from life with Mom, where each of us had his own room and everything had to be neat and tidy. We used to sit up in the sleeping bags, drinking cider or cocoa, playing cards, or just talking. We talked for hours on end. If anyone wanted to sleep, he just fell asleep. Or Muriel would go back to Dad's room. One night in summer when it got very hot, we opened the door on to the balcony, and stuck the ends of the sleeping bags with our heads outside, to be cooler and get some air. In the middle of the night, of course there had to be a storm! I swear I never laughed so much in my life.

Significantly, this was the best period of his relationship with his father as a child, according to Jim. It was when he felt closest to him, when he enjoyed his company most, and when he had the highest regard for him. Earlier, it had been short visits, difficult to arrange because of arguments over money and over access. Later, when his father had teamed up with a divorced woman and her two young children, there was never quite the same easygoing assumption that the two of them could share thoughts—any thoughts—at any time. They went on seeing each other, but less frequently. Ironically, his father's friend, now his wife, used to occupy a large comfortable house with several guest rooms. You had your own bed, your own towel, and no line up for the bathroom. But it lacked something.

The point of this is that, even if you cannot keep your own children "in the style to which they are accustomed," you can still give them and yourself a very good time. Sometimes it is a bit like an adventure, when you have to discuss how each person is going to sleep, where he can keep his clothes, and how it is all going to work out. Children like adventure. Obviously there are limits, beyond which you have to defer to safety, health and hygienic considerations. But loss of a few creature comforts is nothing, by comparison. Your children are almost certainly more adaptable than you are yourself.

Yet some Saturday parents worry, probably through pride as well as anxiety, to be seen to be doing the right thing by their children and by former spouse alike. They put off arranging for long visits until it becomes almost a habit to avoid them. This is to miss a great opportunity for getting your children to know you better and for you to understand them.

Sometimes there is no choice, but a basic rule for making long visits enjoyable is not to try to do too much too quickly. Children of all ages vary enormously in the speed with which they adapt happily to a few days with their other parent. At five or fifteen, there may still be some big problems at the start, which it pays to watch out for. Under five, it is normal for *any* child to feel nervous about being away from his mother—or that person who acts most like his mother—and it is best to avoid lengthy stays (i.e. over two days) until the idea is accepted that life can go on happily in both homes. My own advice is to start with a weekend and work up, whatever your child's or your children's ages may be. This avoids the problem of a child's worry—which is perfectly natural at first—

becoming crystallized into fear that there is no escape. Children remember fear, when the next time comes around. As for worry, fortunately they remember getting over their worries and enjoying whatever distracted them from the problem.

Next, try to be confident about it. In the background, there is probably a *lack* of confidence. In four cases out of five, the parent who has custody will be worrying about the first long visit. Even where there has not been any "tug-of-love" legal battle over custody, there is a persistent fear of losing a child, which finds its outlet in a host of questions about the suitability of the place where the child is to stay, concern over health, eating, and bedtime. When there is an uncertain relationship between the parent with custody and your child, there is a more subtle and insidious fear. This is the suspicion that your child might indeed prefer life at your place; that he might enjoy the company and friendship of your friends or your new spouse; that the values and life style that he develops are going to be affected by yours. This is the fear of long-term loss of control, as opposed to fear of immediate loss. Both are very potent. Sometimes they are justified. Fear communicates itself very quickly to a child, especially to a younger child. Nothing need be said: it is as if a child can sense that more adrenaline is being used for some reason, and he takes it as his cue to become tense. This is why so many children are nervous about long visits, at the beginning. Your task is to show a little understanding, and be patient with tears and changes of mind. Your *confidence* is going to be the strongest argument for soothing anxiety. Words themselves will help, but avoid long explanations: that is the world of logic, not of emotion.

For younger children, it is always better to have some idea of where it is that you are taking them—before they get there. This means that when you arrive there is recognition rather than confusion, disappointment, or a sense of being lost. If you have already shown your child where you live and where there is a little room for him on a short visit, the transition to a long visit is much easier.

Over the age of seven or eight—again, it depends very much on the emotional age of a child, and whether he has acquired confidence in you as a competent parent who really can organize normal life—there is a sense of exploration and adventure about trying something new. If you plan a camping or holiday expedition together, they will enjoy discussing maps, routes, photographs, and different possible locations with you. But don't attempt to spring this kind of trip suddenly on a nervous child who has not got used to the occasional spell of living with you.

Janice has been spending every third weekend with her father for the past five years. During school holidays this is often extended into periods of a week or two weeks. She is now ten years old.

When you meet her at her father's home, she is anxious to make *you* feel at home. (So much for any curiosity on my part as to whether she was comfortable and whether she "fitted in.") Janice is only too anxious to give a guided tour around the apartment, and points out with some pride the features of her own room. She pauses and knocks on her half-brother's door, but this is about the only formality she observes with Roger, the six-year-old son of her father's current marriage.

Janice knows where everything is stored, and how everything works. "Josie and I are going to be painting the kitchen next time I come over," she told me, referring to her father's wife. She is *active* in this household, and feels some pride and responsibility where its looks and comfort are concerned.

The central core of this feeling for the place is her own room. This is a small box-shaped area that doubles as a storage room, and sometimes a work room when Janice is not there. But most of her things are never disturbed. Her bed, the bedspread, the posters on the wall, the soft toys on the window sill, are all dependable objects which she sees each time she returns. In one corner there is a triangular closet space, covered by a curtain which she herself helped choose. This holds an assortment of clothes: others are folded in a small two-drawer cupboard by her bedside.

Two things are important to note here. First, Janice has her own "defensible territory." There is some space that belongs to her— somewhere to which she can retire if she is feeling ill or distressed. Everybody needs something of the kind if they are to feel confident in a new building. The second point is that Janice's space is small, and not in the least luxurious. It was hard to contrive in a small apartment. But her father, together with Josie, saw to it that it *was* contrived, and made into something personal for Janice. Her father told me:

> She has two homes really. I reckon that if a child is in a split home, she deserves to get the best out of two different places. This makes her lucky in a way. She has in fact boasted to other children that she doesn't just have one room, and one set of clothes and toys, but two. She grows up knowing about two kinds of household and having her own stake in each of them. That's twice what "normal" children get.

It is perhaps natural for him to explain to an outsider how *good* everything is, and how happily they all get along with each other. Probably his memory "forgets" the problems that have come and gone. But there is no denying that Janice feels at home here. And I believe that one of the main reasons for this is that nobody has tried to persuade her that this is where she rightfully belongs, so that her mother's place should be seen as all wrong, or inferior by comparison. It is, purely and simply, an alternative. Her father has not tried to claim more for it than that. This explains why Janice has not felt guilty about enjoying herself there, or about describing something nice that she has enjoyed at her mother's. She hasn't been forced into trying to be tactful, with the result that she has been able to concentrate on fitting in, on getting on with Josie and with Roger, and on enjoying herself.

I was unable to meet Janice's mother, but certain signs suggest that she, too, has developed an easygoing attitude towards Janice's having a second home. For example, Janice casually mentioned to Josie a helpful talk she had had with her mother about a problem of how to stitch together some pieces of material being used to make rag dolls: this was a hobby she had been working on with Josie. Swapping comment and advice had become a natural thing. This means that Janice is probably not subjected to feeling guilty, or having to make critical remarks when she returns home after a stay at her father's.

Possibly the big hazard in longer visits is the way in which your child takes to or manages to coexist with your present partner, or your other children. Janice and her father were lucky that she got on well with Josie and Roger. There are some basic points to be made about relationships of this kind in Chapter 8. But here are some guidelines for reducing the friction in the context of long-stay visits.

Everyone has to have some defensible territory, as described in the case history above. This is where you can return to be by yourself for a while, consult a teddy bear or read a book after a difficult encounter.

The rules about such territory have to be understood. Roger knocks on Janice's door, or calls out to her. And vice versa. He knows this is "her place" and he leaves it alone, together with its contents, between Janice's visits. But Janice has to respect what is Roger's too. A little explanation early on avoids a lot of trouble later. In fact, up to the age of about fourteen or fifteen, children rather *like* social rules. They like knowing where they stand. Inevitably, attempts are made by children to gang up on another child when he incurs their displeasure. You can only avoid giving the feeling that "everybody is against me" by being scrupulously fair over this. "Ganging up" includes all joining in criticism of what one child is doing; all laughing at him when he makes a mistake; or all assuming that he is the guilty party when some household crime (like breaking a vase) has been committed. Of course you must enforce rules, tell a child off, stop him doing something dangerous, and tell him when he is wrong. But you must make it clear that the same house rules apply to every child who happens to be there, during a long visit, so that justice is seen to be done.

Avoid competitive situations, or looking for comparisons. If two children are making models, don't offer a prize for the better airplane or ship, unless you intend giving out *two* prizes at the end.

Giving away old, discarded toys or clothes without first asking your resident child's permission is simply asking for trouble. Even if nothing is said at the time, and even if the object in question has not been used for years, plenty remains unsaid. Children who are normally generous see this casual treatment of their property as an invasion; they store away the memory, and often set about making life more difficult for the newcomer.

Displacing a resident child from his bed or from his room is even more dangerous. Sometimes it has to be done. If so, hold a conference, discuss alternatives, and try to get him to agree to the change, or (better still) outline the problem and let him find the best solution.

Nothing binds human beings together so much as having either a common enemy or a common purpose. A useful common enemy may be the family around the corner, or an opposing football team. Another common enemy is boredom. A joint activity, or a joint project to be completed over the few days they are going to be together, can start to build understanding between them. Don't expect anything like friendship to happen in a brief moment. But sometimes, if you can turn their attention on to someone or something away from each other, you make this result far more probable.

If both of them are bored and frustrated, they are very likely to take this out on each other. Prepare a list of possible joint activities as outlined at the end of Chapter 5, with an eye to suggesting and preparing things that can be continued after a break, over a longer period, if they prove popular.

Another antidote to boredom is the television set: Television during a short visit makes little sense. But over a weekend the box can perform two useful functions. It provides a common source of entertainment for two or more children who are wary of each other, and therefore a common language. It also helps dry tears on occasion. However, almost inevitably one of them will be used to longer viewing hours than the other; and/or prefer different programs; and/or be allowed to view shows that are discouraged for the other. You must be prepared to apply your own house rules (if you have any). Institute turns, so that choice of channel gets shared, when there is disagreement. Occasionally the only way to settle a fight is to announce that *you* want to listen to the radio, or the record player, or to watch an entirely different program from anyone else. If you are uncertain whether or not a particular show would be allowed in your child's home, or might frighten them, it is always best to play safe. Going back with nightmares or stories of sex-orgies culled from the screen will not help your child, and may imperil future visits. (This has become, in fact, a *very* common source of complaint about shared custody or access situations.)

Another way of helping young people to adapt to each other is to make it easier for them to see their own long-standing friends for part of the time. "No, you can't have Tony over again, you've got to help look after Brian this weekend" is the kind of prohibition that makes Brian the logical object of hate. Who knows—Brian may in fact hit it off better with Tony than with your other child. Similarly, if Brian wants to and can have a friend of his over as well (even for part of the time), this is more likely to help things work out well. Noisier for you—happier for them. It also helps provide some continuity from their "other" background.

A lot of the fun of having your child at home with you for a while is just being able to be with each other and explore each other's likes and dislikes without having to worry too much about time. Keeping a balance between having interesting things to do and having a relaxed timetable is an art. The more accustomed your child becomes to his second home, and to his role inside it, the less will be the need for distractions. After a while, he will not be so concerned about what to do next; he will just get on with the process of living without bothering about that. When he starts organizing *you,* it is often a good sign that he is settling in. (You have to strike a balance here too, however.)

So that you can relax yourself, and not worry about what might go wrong to the extent that you are too frazzled to enjoy the visit, you should keep a checklist to make sure that you avoid most of the possible sources of disaster. The only way to feel secure is to make everything secure.

The rest of this chapter may read gloomily, but it is intended to save you trouble, and to give you peace of mind.

TO AVOID MAJOR DISASTERS

1 : Check out your house or apartment in advance. It may suit you perfectly, if you live alone or with another adult or with older children. But is it childproof for the age of your child?

For example, are medicines, shaving equipment, garden liquids, alcohol, bleach, antiseptic concentrates, etc., entirely out of reach?

Is there anything in the kitchen that needs explanation (for example that the gas is not self-lighting; that it's an electric cooker and therefore the rings may be very hot even if they are not bright red; etc.)? Or are there too many dangers in the kitchen to allow your child alone there at all? Are your windows, balconies, and staircases safe?

2 : Make sure you have the necessary first-aid equipment and phone numbers of doctors, hospitals and so forth, for you to use quickly and efficiently if you need them. Note that *you* should aim to have *all* medical angles covered, despite the fact that the average home may well ignore a lot of them. But *you* cannot afford to be accused, later, of floundering or losing vital minutes.

3 : Ask regularly for any new medical information that may be important, for example news of specific allergies, or playground cuts and bruises that have been slow to heal. If you are puzzled by something of this kind, call the other parent up *at once:* this communication may be resented, but you have a duty to your child to ask what it is that may be troubling him.

4 : What are the approaches to your house or apartment like? Are there any road hazards that should be pointed out to your child? What degree of freedom is your child allowed on roads at home? Decide whether to follow suit, or whether a particular major road is too dangerous for walking or cycling. With younger children, are you quite sure they cannot get out on the street, unattended?

TO AVOID MINOR DISASTERS

1 : Make a brief inventory of the cases, parcels, and all other separate objects your child brings with him. Run through this list prior to return. (You may *worry* about a missing raincoat, or teddy bear. But your child may be *frantic*. This affects how he's going to look on future visits.)

2 : Ask if there is anything your child needs to do. You can probe (according to age): homework; project preparation; messages or letters to pass on to you; anything to buy for birthdays; etc. Then make sure he has time and opportunity to get this done.

3 : Always try to keep your child's possessions in particular places, in a particular room. Establish order, or he will become confused and will not regard it as a second home. Then make sure he doesn't lose things (difficult, sometimes, depending on his character) or get them "borrowed" by other children.

4 : Make sure he is not frightened by anything. Go hand in hand with him into dark corners, if you are concerned about this; equip him with a flashlight. You *know* your place; he may not. Similarly, is he frightened by the sound of the toilet? Don't laugh. Young children are often alarmed by them. And make sure that all locks, bolts, and other closures are either easy to use or forbidden and out of range: nothing is so terrifying as discovering that you are locked in.

5 : You should also take precautions against bedtime fears. Your child may have certain bedtime rituals that are crucial to his confidence, for example the door left open, a light left on outside, a reminder of where the bathroom is in case he needs it during the night, etc. Find out what is needed, and supply it.

6 : Make out a list together of foods especially liked and foods disliked. (You don't need to give way to every whim, but there is no earthly reason why somebody who hates spinach should be faced with it.) Do this at the *start* of a long visit—while the shops are still open.

7 : Suppose your child takes away with him something that belongs to your home. Before wading into the attack, ask yourself what this means. When young children steal, they usually feel the need for more affection. Often they rather want to be found out, and therefore bungle the job. If it's money or candy, this is usually a safe diagnosis: be firm, but understanding. Take it as the moment to get closer, spend more time together, and talk things through quietly. If it's more like a momento, this is in fact rather flattering. He wants, symbolically, a piece of *you* to take away. Next time, anticipate this by suggesting something that he could take back to fix, repair, polish or clean. But make sure it's something unimportant to the fabric of your house, because you might not see it again.

7: When the Saturday Parent Is the Mother

In more than four cases out of five, the practice in most English-speaking countries is to grant custody of a child to the mother, where this is contested. This was not always the case. The "guilty party" in divorce cases used to have a very difficult time establishing why they should have custody, whichever sex they were. Research into the effects of separation from the mother during the forties and fifties made it clear that particularly for young children it was a dangerous policy to sever the link between mother and child. This led to a general relaxation of policy, including consideration of whether the best place for a child to be had anything to do whatever with events preceding a marriage breakdown. Lawyers who were more concerned with human feelings made comments like this one: "When a man has to leave his young children it is painful, but a woman may totally collapse." The current moved decisively in the direction of awarding custody in nearly all cases to the mother, once account had been taken of children's ages.

But this presupposed two things. First, that the mother was more maternal than the father. Second, that the role she chose automatically was to stay at home and look after children. Both of these points may or may not be valid in any particular situation. Variations in make-up, interest, and ambition are infinite. The courts are really only beginning to take into account the change of perspective that this demands.

The pendulum has begun to swing back. The proportion of cases where custody is awarded to the father is still a minority (a small minority where the child is under six), but the figure has been rising since 1972. The well-known case of Dr. Leo Salk, the New York psychologist who successfully contested the initial custody award after his divorce, led many to a re-examination of the arguments that could apply. Social workers will tell you that they often encountered serious problems caused by automatic custody awards where the mother is ill equipped emotionally, physically, intellectually, or materially to manage children on her own. But it isn't easy for a court to determine degree of interest, ability at looking after children, and so forth.

Joint custody, where children may be growing up in two separate households, attracted more attention in the seventies as a solution that can sometimes benefit everyone.

In any event, there are more and more Saturday parents nowadays who are women. In some cases they probably still suffer from a kind of stigma that a man might escape. Traditionally minded people may speculate how—if she is a "real" mother—she can enjoy life away from her children. This kind of criticism is sexist in nature, and mercifully it is gradually on the way out. But it still persists. I mention it because it is an extra, or rather an intensified, pressure on this kind of Saturday parent. As such it may increase the emotional problems associated with periodic visiting. To have successful, rewarding visits for child and parent you should recognize these problems, and then nudge them to one side.

If you feel guilty it is better to come to terms with it than to deny that you could feel anything of the kind. It is too easy to go to the opposite extreme as a kind of pose, for your own comfort. Nobody is immune from criticism or doubt, if they are a human being. Sometimes it can be harder to be natural and show that you are concerned for your child despite the fact that you are convinced it is better for everyone if you lead your own life in a separate household. These two things are perfectly consistent, provided you believe them to be so. You don't need an aggressive mask of indifference simply because society believes you are inconsistent. You want your child, presumably, to appreciate you for who you really are. You have to show him more than the mask.

AR is at university. He has a very close relationship with his father. He is fond of his mother. He is glad they kept up contact—which continues—although his main recollections are negative.

> I always hated meeting my mother. My father used to take me into this hotel and point across the groups of chairs and tables where people were having lunch. I used to go over to the group where I could see my mother with her friends. She would open her arms and cry, "Tony! Darling! How wonderful to see you!" Without pausing for breath, she used to continue her conversation with whoever was with her while actually kissing me. Then I was sat down on a chair, and someone would order an extra cup and a plate. She hardly ever said anything else to me the whole time I was there. Except of course for:
>
> "How are you getting on at school, then, Tony?"
>
> "Oh, fine thanks."
>
> There were usually three or four other qeople, all chatting away. I was stuffed full of egg salad sandwiches and cakes, while they rabbited on about the people they knew and the parties they had enjoyed. Once mother got very angry with me because I was "looking like a sick moon-calf." One of her friends took my arm and we went out for a walk.
>
> When I was about twelve, I said I wasn't going to go any more. After a week or two B (my father) told me to bite the bullet and try one more time. I felt tougher by then. I went up to her, and said, "Hello, how've you been, and are we going to say anything to each other?" She burst into tears and this made me feel awful. Her friends disappeared, and we went up to her room. She said she'd felt very bad about leaving me, and this was just "her way." She wasn't such a cold-blooded person after all. We were both embarrassed. We didn't have any words to use with each other. But we got to meeting up for a show or a meal every now and then. It was better afterwards.

The Saturday parent in this case has been analyzed by her intelligent son as suffering basically from guilt. This caused her to parade him in front of her friends as a casual social acquaintance, without running any risk of showing emotion. This she was afraid to do. When he came up and demanded something closer she was ill prepared for it. Not knowing much about her real self, he was stunned by her reaction.

Forcing a kind of casual atmosphere may sometimes be necessary. But insisting on an adult unemotional front as a basis for visiting shows very little consideration for what may be going on in your child's mind. If he hasn't seen you for, say, two weeks, he is going to want something more cosy than egg salad sandwiches. He or she might seem casual too, at first. But this is only skin-deep.

Some mothers are afraid of showing emotion from another point of view. If they become too deeply entangled with their children, they fear this might handicap the child—*either* by making it harder for him to get along without her when they are not together *or* by preventing a good relationship developing with his stepmother. This is a question of degree. Certainly any mother can, if she is determined, turn each visit into a soggy, semi-tragic scene, thereby making life harder for the children between times. But the natural element between a mother and child is love. There should be evidence of this, spontaneous not contrived, when they meet. Otherwise your child feels two things: that you are always denying him something and that mothers in general tend to be like that. By showing affection you make the between times easier, not more difficult.

There are also case histories of mothers who in fact *dislike* their children. They feel, however, duty-bound to go and see them once in a while. Whether they can get round this dislike and provide and enjoy a satisfying relationship depends very much on how much of an imposition they feel it is and on how much conviction they get that they are supplying something individual that their child would not get otherwise.

One such mother works for an airline. Her child has two Saturday parents, in fact. From an early age she has been brought up by her grandmother. Liz, now five, sees her father every two weeks, and stays the weekend with him. At intervals largely dictated by the airline's schedules, her mother comes back to see her too. Her mother is frank about why she chose this life:

> I like seeing Liz now and then. When I want to. I'd never have got married if I hadn't been pregnant, and I suppose I hold it against her in a way. But I'm not much good with kids in any case. Liz is far better off with her gran. If I have to be looking after her for longer than a day or two, I go right out of my mind. I shout at her, and shake her up and down. This way it's much better. We have fun together, and I tell her stories.

According to the grandmother, Liz enjoys seeing her mother. But she gave me to understand that she herself was the *real* mother, whatever Liz might call her. That is as it may be. The point is that there is a positive relationship between Liz and no less than three different people, who are living different lives. Liz seems cheerful, intelligent, and makes friends easily with other children. The successful relationship with her mother almost certainly depends on their meetings not being extended beyond the point of tolerance. Nobody can *make* themselves more maternal simply by repeating in a mirror what they are told they should be like.

A classic problem of the mother who is separated from her children is a feeling that where their health is concerned something is being done wrong. This stems from an instinct that only the real mother has the intuition to realize when and how her child really needs some physical aid. This intuition can be totally wrong, as many false alarms in so-called "normal" families prove every day. But people tend to remember the times that the intuitive feeling was right.

This leads to approaching each visit in a critical frame of mind. If you have this conviction you ask yourself as you are walking up to the front door: "What is going to be wrong this time? Will he be wearing warm enough clothing? Will he still have a snuffle in his nose? Has he been getting enough to eat? Has he been eating the right things? I'll ask him what he had for breakfast this morning, and it's ten to one they forgot to give him his wheatgerm . . . ."

If you find that on each visit you are levelling complaints about clothing, food, uncombed hair, etc., step back for a moment and think about each of these things again. How much of it is really necessary, and how much is simply what you feel to be normal and desirable? What is a genuine disadvantage, and what is common to most children anyway? Ex-husbands are typically (but not invariably) more relaxed about how much gleam there should be on a child's teeth and leather shoes. Are you in fact complaining about matters of opinion and style, or something more important? Why not be more selective where battlegrounds are concerned? Forget the shoes, for example, and concentrate on the teeth. That way you may be listened to more often.

Any family, married or split, will go through phases when the child chooses not to look after his hair; not to allow the holes in his jeans to be sewn or patched; to despise traditional suburban footwear; to eat junk food, and plenty of it; to experiment with cigarettes. The list is endless. If you are deeply concerned that your child is sporting some of these insignia, reflect that he is actually joining the majority of his peer group. Children have a compulsive need to join that majority, which transcends anything that their fathers, stepmothers, or the absence of their "real" mothers may have been encouraging or allowing. If you are on the look-out for evidence of mismanagement, you will surely find it. Concentrate instead on those things which might be really important.

Forget what your child has been eating. Does he look in good shape? Is he strong? Is he healthy, or flabby? Is there any sign of squinting, or bad hearing, or skin trouble? This kind of thing is worth noticing. You may be able to help.

But don't turn each meeting into a health and welfare check. You are not Florence Nightingale doing her rounds. You want to be associated with some fun, some relaxation, and a change of pace—not just the smell of cough drops.

Having found a real problem, you need to decide how to approach it. Don't expect to be thanked for your trouble, or to have a gold star pinned to your chest. And keep an open mind as to whether the problem has already been noted at home. There are two typical responses you might get. Each of them needs interpretation. The first is:

"I know about that. It's been obvious a long time. Dr. K prescribed a course of treatment. We've been following it. A specialist at the hospital confirmed that we were doing the right thing."

This means, in fact, that something has been done, and it is worrying because nothing has improved. It is a warning only to make practical suggestions.

The second response is:

"Of course I know about that: Do you think I haven't noticed? Anyway, it's been dealt with. So shut up."

This means that it had not been noticed at all. You have made the other parent feel guilty, and alarmed him sufficiently to make sure that he will contact a doctor. Do not make any further suggestions, practical or otherwise, until he has had a chance to sort something out.

Naturally it is irritating to have to interpret, instead of taking things at face value. But you must if you want to read the situation accurately. Only if you are genuinely asked for your opinion can you be reasonably certain that you can discuss your child's problems objectively and dispassionately. Watch out for this sign, because it tells you that the period of double talk is over. Unless, that is, you exploit the situation to raise a lot of other troubles.

Some mothers cannot stop themselves. They take the matter directly into their own hands. They devote part of their access visits to making sure that their child sees a second doctor, a second dentist, a second orthodontist, etc. This is disastrous, except in circumstances where an accident has happened during your visit, for two reasons. First, your interference will be strongly resented. Your opinion will be studiously ignored *even when* you have something important to bring to people's notice. Second, your child's attitude towards the problem becomes more intense. Some children will prolong their symptoms (consciously or unconsciously) to prolong the extra attention they get. Others may become anxious that they are causing more friction between their parents because of their health problem. All will regard the visits they get as stressful, rather than enjoyable.

Suppose you suspect a fracture where it is assumed there is only a sprain. You will gain far more by talking directly to the father or the stepmother in the following terms:

"Look, I know you must have thought of this, but I've seen something like this before, and wouldn't it be better if we all went down to the X-ray unit at the hospital, just to make sure?"

What you are doing is *involving* them. You may not enjoy it, but you will help your child more that way. It shows that you prefer to co-operate, rather than wading in like a crusading angel. Even if you are wrong about the fracture, they will listen to you more indulgently the next time.

The other pitfall to avoid is delaying to the point where you despair of the home team ever noticing what you have noticed, and doing something about it. Your anxiety builds up to bursting before you finally bring it to people's attention. What was to have been a normal, peaceful handover on the doorstep after a visit turns into this:

> "Is anything wrong? Why are you looking at me like that?"
> "Can't you *see* that his shoes are too tight? Does he have to become a cripple for the rest of his life?" (Tears)
> "Oh, well. Better do something, then." (Mutters, takes child inside, slams door.)

A mother, who was not very proud of this scene in retrospect, described it to me. She used to take her boy, then aged seven, to a swimming pool when they met, and she noticed that certain of his toes were red and sore. After examining his sandals against his feet, she had asked him to tell his father they were too small now, but either he had not wanted to or he had forgotten. About a month went by without her saying anything more. Then the emotional dam burst.

Her son got new sandals all right, but he also had to witness this bizarre scene which those who have managed to preserve good communications after divorce will probably never understand. It was probably a reminder of past rows, before the break-up. Once again it probably made him wonder at least for a moment whether he wasn't destined to be the root cause of his family's rift.

Saying something at an early stage brings the risk of being accused of fussing. But that depends on how you go about it. And it's not as harmful as a big blow-up later.

This begs a question, of course. Some Saturday parents—and *not* just mothers—may actually have an urge to provoke a scene of the kind just described. They are still spoiling for a fight, not necessarily knowing about this. Sore toes on a child's feet become an opportunity, then. If you have enough control to be able to choose, this is a bad choice of battleground. If you suspect something similar in yourself, think about the most recent unpleasant scenes you have had and ask yourself directly if you may not have been enjoying them, at least in part.

Less tangible, but probably more taxing to you emotionally, is the mental state of your child—how he is developing socially, morally, intellectually, while you are absent from him. Your absence may be part of your concern; there is also the presence of other people, possibly the "other woman," in your child's everyday life. You ask yourself how this is going to work out and, while sometimes you may feel it is for the best, you have some anxiety that he should retain something that is yours, personally, in his make-up.

This is perfectly natural. But if you are really going to be an influence, you have to do so positively. In the time that you are together with him, you should show your child that you are the person that you are: somebody who can enjoy life, while having certain standards and feeling certain responsibilities. If you moralize half the time, or inquire anxiously about school work, or (worse, and sometimes fatal) criticize your ex-husband's new partner or their way of doing things, then you will gradually lose any effectiveness you had, since he will hear you without listening. But if you are prepared to listen to *him,* sometimes (particularly if he is entering his teens), you might even find yourself the only person to whom he feels he can express his point of view. You may not agree with him always, but at least you are *there*.

Think for a moment about your child with your ex-husband's new partner (whether she is an official stepmother or not). In nearly every interview with a mother who is absent from her former home, the same kind of thing comes up: she tells me there are a number of things for which she admires her husband's new partner, but these are usually generalities (for example she gets on well with the ex-husband, has a lot of determination, etc.) Entering into detail, she tells me about the *mistakes* the other has made. The open-minded modern outlook may be claimed, but it does not stand up to much scrutiny. This should be recognized, not concealed.

A read through my interview transcripts convinces me that the stepmother cannot in fact do the right thing. If the child is happy living with her, I am told she has "brainwashed" him successfully, or that she has "been too permissive." Occasionally such a person is said to have "spoiled him rotten." If on the other hand he is unhappy with her, well, what can one expect with someone who cares only for herself, and is too house-proud, too repressive?

Whatever is going on there is bound to be difference in some way or other from the pattern that would have been established in your own household. Whatever is different strikes you as being wrong for someone who was once part of you. This is natural. If you come to terms with this fact, you can start to sort out the important from the incidental.

When you visit your child, or take him home for the weekend, it is pointless to regard it as an opportunity to reshape his social values. You don't have the time. You can point out that there are certain rules in your home, and maybe some different priorities too. This is simply living what you are. But your child needs to adapt to the situations he most often meets. He may learn to talk about different things when he is with you, and he may start assessing things by asking different questions. But this is because you have changed the milieu, briefly, and made it an interesting, perhaps a challenging, one. You are in effect extending his repertoire, not reshaping him as a person. What you are doing is fine—but do not pitch your expectations too high, in terms of long-lasting effect.

You may find that your child is rude or badly-behaved according to your standards. You should certainly stop him from doing anything that you believe is antisocial while he is with you. Before you blame the other parties, you should reflect that it may be causing them some anguish too. Instead of blaming one another, you could accomplish far more by getting together some time to talk over the problem.

The most relaxed absent mothers that I have met have been able to keep up contact with their ex-husband, and with his partner, to discuss how their children are getting on, what the problems are, whether they are showing any new interests or talents, and how they can best be helped. How this is accomplished varies a lot. One mother meets the stepmother regularly because she finds they can talk more easily by themselves and that they "talk more to the point." Some teachers find that, when separated parents turn up for interviews at their child's school, they linger to sort out a number of items in a useful way. The school setting is good in a way because it provides neutral ground. Be assured that it is not just couples who attend those meetings nowadays. In time past, when society tried its hardest to keep "exes" apart, perhaps it was so. But not now. Another absent mother has dinner at an Italian restaurant every month with her ex-husband and his wife. They talk about schools, holiday plans, their daughter's interest and friends, and of course any problems about time schedules for pick-ups, and any questions about health and discipline that have come up.

It often seems more difficult to establish this kind of relaxed communication where the Saturday parent is the mother. It is a mistake to try to arrange meetings of this kind with your ex-husband only, as if his partner did not exist or did not have anything to contribute. This is simply asking for trouble. Nor does it make sense to try to have a friendly meeting about your child when there may be a battle raging about money. The problem then is to avoid raising the suspicion that every point made in the conversation—whether about clothing, food preferences or holidays—is actually a veiled attempt to add to the propaganda about how much more money should be given or received. Otherwise it makes a lot of sense to get into the habit of a periodic meeting (preferably *without* your child there, since it may encourage him to dramatize his feelings or his problems if he knows that he is the center of attention for an hour or so). The main benefit is to be able to anticipate difficulties before they arise. If you suddenly meet your child with his arm in a sling, it does something to you. If you've been told about it beforehand, and if you've been told that the X-rays show a straightforward fracture with no complications, it will be far less of a shock. The other kind of benefit is best described by a small anecdote, which is fairly typical of a situation where communications are good.

Judy was due to pick up her two children one weekday after school, to take them with her to act as helpers in a cooking class that she ran. Her car broke down. She had no hesitation in calling her children's stepmother and asking her to break the news gently that the promised treat would not take place.

Stella, the stepmother, knew the background, including the fact that Judy's car had been making peculiar noises. She knew also how much the children had been looking forward to helping, and to finishing off leftovers. She drove the children herself to the night school, so they would be there on time, and later their father picked them up.

Very simple, really, Those who *do* communicate with their ex-husbands find this story utterly banal. Their reaction tends to be "Well? What would you expect?" They don't know how lucky or how sensible they are. At the same time, another absent mother to whom I told the story commented that the people "must be very strange indeed" if they can take things "so coolly." But think of the advantages of making yourself a little more cool.

Communication also helps you understand a little better what your child is saying to you.

> I was shocked when my daughter said to me one Sunday afternoon that she never wanted to go back to her father again. She insisted that she was desperately unhappy. [Norma, the daughter, was ten at this time, and had been living with her father for five years. A year previously, he had remarried.] She cried, and she refused to go home. I tried to get at what she was unhappy about, but I just got a jumbled reply.
>
> The best thing to do seemed to be to leave her at my home while I spoke to her father and his wife. They didn't know exactly what to make of it either, and we agreed that Norma should stay the night at my place. She needed a lot of hugging, and she slept badly. Once she asked me, out of the blue, if the police would follow her to my home. The next day I got a phone call from Alex (the stepmother) to say she thought she knew what the problem was. We met again, and she told me what she had got from her own daughter, Marian [Marian was 12]. Apparently Norma had accepted a dare at school and she took something from a store. Marian had told her the police would surely be after her if they found out. We agreed Norma had had enough punishment, of a kind, and Marian said she was sorry for frightening her. Her father helped her write a letter to the store manager (conscience money enclosed), and convinced her that would be the end of it.

One point about this episode in Norma's life is that it is extremely common (more so, perhaps, than many parents would care to admit). In the context of split home, a common situation can become interpreted as something much more serious—evidence, perhaps of mistreatment by the stepmother, or being led astray. If you can talk things over, calmly, *before* such a problem arises, you can understand what is going on and act accordingly.

To underline the moral: the mother in this case does not in fact get on particularly well with Alex, resents her for being the prime cause of her marriage breakdown, and finds it hard to control her feelings when they are together. But from time to time she forces herself to make the effort. "The first time," she tells me, "was the worst." Nowadays, she feels it is just common sense.

The initiative may come from the other side. A man I know was staggered when his second wife suggested they should get together with his first wife to talk about the health and school problems that their daughter was experiencing. (The mother did not have custody.) "And I think Andy [the mother's long-standing male companion] should come too."

The father's reply was "Oh my God!"

But she insisted: "If you don't ask them, I will. We'll go somewhere and have dinner."

The mother also said "Oh my God" when the suggestion was made on the telephone. But she was too surprised to refuse. Andy, interestingly, thought it was a very good idea. At the first meeting, they filled an ashtray within the first twenty minutes. But the more they talked about the child, the more they realized they were each looking at her and her problems from a slightly different viewpoint, and with different information. This was no help to the child, and it was no help to them in getting a better idea of how to help her with her allergies. Now they knew more. And, amazingly, they developed some respect for what the other parties were suggesting, and trying to do.

"When I put the receiver down I thought it a stupid idea," the mother admitted. "But now I'm glad I wasn't given time to think it over."

There are times when an absent mother will feel that she is being frozen out. This is sometimes a natural by-product of her child's growing up and having different interests. Sometimes, the stepmother may make a big impression on the child, who will increasingly look to her for help, ideas, fun, and even love. When this occurs, it is hard to tell yourself this is probably a good thing. The worst you can do is to criticize your child for it. Blaming him, blaming the stepmother, looking sour—none of this makes sense, although you may feel a strong imuplse to do all three. If you appeal to your child's sense of loyalty, he will not love you for it. That way, he will increasingly associate *you* with problems, with tearful scenes, and a need to behave in a way that is different from his basic inclination. If you stress what he owes to you, you risk signifying to him a kind of joyless obligation. Whether you like it or not, if he is a normal child, he will want to have a good time *both* when he is with you *and* when he is in his other home. If you sense that the pendulum of affection is swinging the other way, away from you, then think long-term, not short-term. The pendulum will swing back, more than likely.

A short-term answer would be to get angry, and demand your parental respect and devotion. This may win the battle but certainly loses the war. Another short-term answer is to think of counter-balancing the magnetism exerted by the other woman through presents or expensive trips. The older the child, and the more intelligent he is, the quicker he will see through this kind of tactic. Anyway, gifts come and go: does anybody, who is not in love for the first time, stop and contemplate a watch every hour of the day and think about the person who gave it? Trips are a bit different because they offer the opportunity to share thoughts and get to know someone rather better. But you must make use of it for that purpose if you organize one. The fact that you took him skiing counts for very little in the end. The memory of your admiration of how he got on, and perhaps the way you looked after his sprain, could be positive, over a period of time.

What you *can* do, if you feel you are losing out, is ask yourself how restrictive you are. Don't compromise your beliefs or ideals, but see if there isn't some way in which you may be unnecessarily cramping his style each time you get together. Do you involve his friends in your visits? Can he talk to you about them without his getting embarrassed or your getting bored? These may be things to adjust. What you can continue to do is to be patient and affectionate. In the long term, those things are respected.

The other thing that costs less than you think is to make yourself a little more interesting, and unpredictable. The more your child can accurately forecast what your suggestions for a visit or a weekend are going to be, the more he is inclined to regard you as being in a rut. Admittedly, it is always easier to be a more interesting character if you have a lot of money and a lot of free time, to let you indulge in scuba diving, free-fall parachuting, or whatever captures a youngster's imagination. But money isn't everything. If you can come up with new friends, including some in his age group; new walks to try out; new recipes to prepare together; new things to collect; new interests that happen to fit in with preferred subjects at school—then you can intensify your own magnetism. Or very simply, do as one Saturday parent said she had done, to shake up her daughter's ideas about her. "We're going to the movies," she had said. "I'm curious about the new rock film." Caught off guard, her daughter had replied, "Oh—do you think you should?"

At the heart of it all lies the fact that if you are a pleasant person to be with then they will enjoy being with you. If they are curious about you, rather than pitying you as a tragic figure, that makes you much more pleasant to be with. This means a gradual transition, which can be more difficult for mothers than for fathers, between being a mother and being a companion as the child grows older. Nobody enjoys a companion who complains all the time, even if she has plenty to complain about. Everyone prizes and admires a companion who takes the trouble to find out what's on *their* minds, and who retains a capacity for cheerfulness.

A different and altogether more serious kind of freezing-out happens when an ex-husband attempts to stop your contact with your child. This is dealt with more fully in the last chapter of this book, but a word is appropriate here. You cannot assume that because you *are* the mother the law will treat you differently than if it was a father who was being frozen out. You have to pursue your case doggedly and patiently. You should watch for these opportunities to help yourself:

1 : Be conciliatory, and reach a compromise. If you keep a foot in the door, you can widen the aperture later. Mobilize the moral drive of relatives, his as well as your own, and any friends you have in common. Let them know about your attempts to keep in touch with your child (without hysterics) even if it embarrasses them a bit.

2 : Get your children to ask to see you. Set up a regular time for phoning, with reversed charges if necessary. Teach them to use a payphone. Rehearse this *during* visits, if possible, to get them used to the procedure.

3 : If necessary, keep evidence of any message or act that was calculated to mislead you or the law about your visiting, and likewise anything that was actually against the law.

8: Meet My New Friend

In a very simple world, husband and wife would simply part company and remain single units. Thereafter, whichever one did not have custody of their child would become a Saturday parent and make periodic visits. No other people are involved, so that the only relationships to consider are those between the members of the original family.

Life is not like that. This much should be obvious from many of the case histories in this book. Other people intrude. Sometimes they even become more significant than the parents in the eyes of the child. But whatever happens, successful contact with the absent parent often depends in large measure on the way such newcomers are perceived, and what their reations are like.

Many complex relationships are possible. This chapter tackles questions concerning each of the new people who are likely to come on the scene. They are: the "other" woman or man; the "new daddy" (or mom); new brothers and sisters; and the extended family.

THE "OTHER" WOMAN OR MAN

Very often when families split up there is someone who is regarded as being at least partly responsible for getting the husband to leave home, or—if she appears later—for keeping him away. There is also her male counterpart, the other man. Most of what I say here applies to both.

Occasionally such a person does not actually exist, but is believed to do so. A casual acquaintance may then find herself cast in this role, rather to her surprise, and receiving odd looks from the child who has been warned at home about her.

The precise status of the other woman is often in doubt. Marriage as such has to be deferred until after divorce. But a continuous relationship may exist which could be regarded either as permanent or open-ended, depending on how the individuals feel at the time, or view their prospects of making it work.

The main thing your child will try to decide about your new friend is simply this: does this person seem to be a short-term or a long-term attachment to your life? Official titles like "friend" or "wife" may not mean much. From experience your child knows this, or senses it. What matters is for him to know whether this is someone to be treated on a casual basis or as an established part of your life. After that, come questions like the following: "Should I be jealous of the attention and love this person gets? Is this a desirable extension of my mother's or father's life?"

Whatever he regards as temporary, your child may ignore. If he is still at the age when he maintains a hope of effecting a reconciliation between his parents, he may well *choose* to ignore your friend, whatever the indications. When this happens, he is telling himself, and you, "This one's only passing through, right?" If he has gone beyond the point of trying to mend the old marriage, your child may try one of two things. The first is to guide your choice. The second is to establish a particular kind of relationship between himself and your friend, to ensure that she joins the magic circle on the child's terms. This usually means trying to share your attention in equal measure, and may involve anxiety over private jokes or references that you have with each other that exclude him. This is natural, and there are compromises to be made—on both sides. It is the matchmaking spirit that tends to cause most of the problems.

Your child feels some responsibility for you. This may surprise you. But reflect: a child in a single-parent home usually develops certain feelings of added responsibility towards that parent. (Some can handle this burden better than others.) But he will probably show a similar concern about *you*. Faced with someone who seems to be temporary, then, he will typically try either to reinforce or to torpedo the chances of permanent attachment. He will see things more in black and white than you will. Influencing the outcome can take several forms. The classical tactics for driving a newcomer away are spiders in their shoes, frogs in the bed, and pulling faces each time the newcomer speaks. But many children are more subtle in their approach. Some look suspiciously at anything the newcomer cooks or brings as a treat. Others change the conversation suddenly to recall an old family holiday, a former family friend, or a past family joke. This is much harder to withstand, however unpleasant the frogs.

During this period, any attempt by the newcomer to issue a command or a warning, or even to suggest a change of plan, meets stiff resistance. Rather than be seen to listen, obey, or not obey, your child may simply pretend not to hear, or leave the room, or start his own private game. Acknowledging that such a person has a right to command or warn is more alarming to him than the command or the warning itself. This would be tantamount to condoning the crucial move from temporary to permanent.

But encouragement happens too. This may mean hugs, smiles, and evidence of a kind of "crush" on the fortunate person. Sometimes it is almost as if your child is trying to show you how you should be treating her. But encouraging behavior is not always straightforward. It can be very bizarre. This is more typical when a child has mixed feelings towards the newcomer, including resentment, liking, and guilt about that liking. Your child may then show approval of your choice by starting a mild argument and escalating it into horseplay. This has to be stopped before clothes get torn or somebody gets hurt. There are tears, and you tell the child off. You may well ask yourself, "What has he got against her? They seemed to be getting on so well." But that's just it. The way your child sees that your relationship can be strengthened is by breaking down a few barriers. He fights, says he's sorry, and makes it up again. This may mean cuddling, and more obvious emotion than there had been before. Naturally, this kind of behavior imposes a strain. But it is less exasperating if you work out what it may mean.

If a newcomer who is regarded as temporary presumes too far too quickly, there is often a gap between the two that cannot be easily bridged. The chances of this are greatest in adolescence, when pride and sensibility are easily ruffled. Later on, your child and your friend may tell the world, "We just never got on." What this *usually* means is that the level of pride, possibly on both sides, was misjudged. It takes a lot of self-confidence to say, "I seem to have made a bad start: could we please begin again?" Discipline is the most obvious area in which to "presume too far." You will find this problem easier if you decide on a few rules, and make them understood. Don't rely on a child's intuition.

You and your friend may be in the full flush of a beautiful relationship, convinced that it will be permanent. Your child cannot know all about this, particularly if he doesn't see you all that often or has seen you with *other* new friends, who turned out to be only temporary. He cannot then be expected to react obediently to the newcomer without any advance groundwork. Look at it from his point of view: why on earth should he suddenly start taking orders from somebody he barely knows, when you haven't told him anything about your rules, or your intentions? He's not a doormat, after all. Talk to your child a little, about what's going on. No running commentary is required. It is in fact very unlikely that he will repeat much of it when he gets home. You will find a closer harmony in your household if you indicate the main drift of your feelings. If you find later that you made a mistake, tell him that too. He will respect you more for it than if you keep him totally in the dark.

At some point, you will need to be clear about delegated authority. Here is one example: "I'm the big boss in this house, Jenny, you know that." His daughter, aged four, had successfully been playing one adult off against the other. "Now Peggy, over there, is the little boss. And when the little boss says it's time to go and have your bath, you go *straight* upstairs to the bathroom. Have you got that, young lady?"

This may be too sexist for some, I realize. There is no reason why a woman should not be a "big boss" and a man a "little boss." I agree wholeheartedly that equal trust and respect between the sexes is better in children's upbringing than stereotyped roles. But children understand delegated authority, and respond to it. They dislike a vacuum, and they want to know that there are some rules around. When they are confronted by equal units, one of whom they know very well and the other hardly at all, it helps them if you supply the rules for a simple archaic family group. Then you may pursue the egalitarian bit at your leisure.

It won't all sink in at first. Children are always curious about behavior thresholds, too. There is sometimes a compulsion to find out how far they can go with somebody, or in a new system. Be prepared to make the same speech more than once, and be clear and consistent. It helps a great deal if Peggy (see above) can smile, and give a kind of salute. You both need to show that the group structure you are working out contains enjoyment as well as discipline.

A last word on this subject is important. No new friend should ever dole out physical punishment to your child (whatever your thoughts on the matter) before the relationship is so close that your child hugs and kisses her spontaneously. This is the only way to make sure that their relationship stands a chance. Otherwise, sooner or later, your child will certainly take his revenge. Many would suggest that you avoid physical punishment altogether anyway—but that is not the subject of this book, although I endorse that view.

At some point a discussion between your child and your new partner has got to be engineered *without you present*. That way they will find out much more about each other as individuals. Don't rush the scene. But don't be so nervous that you keep putting it off. If you are present yourself, you will feel an irresistible impulse to get involved, which will in fact prevent them from getting an understanding going.

Here is an example that shows why this is important.

Martin (aged eight) was very cold toward his father's new wife, Michèle. It was their first short holiday together as a trio. Michèle had gone out of her way to provide nice food, treats, opportunities for Martin to say what he wanted, and games to play. But he kept avoiding her eyes, and was unable to smile back. He did not enjoy himself much, although with his father around he could concentrate on physical play with him, and avoid having much to do with his stepmother. He answered her questions briefly and politely, but volunteered nothing.

Wisely, Michèle persuaded her husband to go out of the house one morning, to keep him from hovering near. "Just give us an hour," she said. She asked Martin to dry the breakfast dishes and help prepare sandwiches for a picnic when that was finished. Then they sat down over orange juice and cookies. Talking while sharing an activity is always easier than settling down deliberately "to have a little talk, you and I."

Even so, Michèle had to cast several conversational lines into the stream before she felt a tug on one of them.

"Are you going to write that postcard to your mom this morning? You know, the one you bought yesterday."

"Perhaps. I don't know what to write on it really."

"Hm. You could say something about the marineland we went to, with the seals and the walrus."

Martin seemed unconvinced. He muttered that he was forbidden to say anything about her, Michèle, or anything that they did together.

"Why not just say, 'Daddy and I saw Marineland?' " Michèle suggested. "It's the truth, and you're not saying anything about me."

Martin thought this a good idea, and thanked her.

"Don't say if you don't want to, but, er, why are you not supposed to mention me, Martin?"

He was relieved to talk about it. It was quite a load to carry around silently. "Because you're a horrible person who is very beautiful but you tempted Daddy away, and stole him from us." This sounded a little mechanical, like a litany.

"I see," Michèle commented as brightly as she could. "Tell me, do you think I'm as bad as all that?"

They looked at each other eye to eye for practically the first time. Suddenly they both started laughing.

"No, you're not," he decided.

"As for the 'beautiful' bit, I can look like a monkey if I want to—watch!"

Martin admired her imitation, laughed a lot, and told her she was indeed very ugly.

When Martin's father returned, the atmosphere seemed totally changed. Do not suppose that everything went smoothly after that. It seldom does. But it was an important stage. They suddenly knew much more about each other. Martin could relax, and enjoy the holiday more. The same goes for Michèle.

A question often debated is whether the children of the parent without custody should attend the wedding, if that parent marries again. (There is more emotion behind the question when the children have already attended the custodial parent's second wedding.) There are no hard and fast rules. I believe it depends on three questions.

First, does your child have an enjoyable time with your future spouse? Can they be said to have a close relationship?

Second, is it likely your child will miss the event, and regret not being invited?

Third, a child at a parent's wedding (whatever the circumstances) often feels out of things. Is there somebody or some group of people who can be relied on to give your child time and attention, and good company?

If the answer is "yes" in every case, you should certainly ask your child to come. If there is a mixture of "yes" and "no," you have to weigh the factors and use your judgment. Unless your children are of widely varying ages, you should ask both or all if they would like to attend.

Should any child not wish to come, that should be the end of the discussion. Forcing the issue is pointless.

You may be told that the event will be "very disturbing" for your child. But you should be the judge of that, and you should ask your child direct.

Before such an event, there is the well-known situation where a former spouse forbids any meeting between your child and your partner unless and until you are married. This happens less now than it used to do. But many second marriages are probably precipitated by this demand, so that they take place sooner than they would have done otherwise. Assuming you do *not* wish to be rushed, what do you do? First, there is no legal reason why you should not continue seeing your child with or without your partner. Something like a criminal record might have to be paraded in court before access was judged to be conditional on never meeting a particular person.

You may prefer to get to know somebody really well before arranging a meeting with your children, but this is your personal choice.

If you are having problems anyway over fixing up access, you may decide it is better not to antagonize your ex-spouse, and keep your visits just between you and the child. But beware of two points. If you are seen to go along with the demand at the outset, you will be accused of treachery (or worse) later on, when you eventually feel it is high time your child and your partner met each other. An older child may be pressing for this. It is also a limiting situation: how are you going to move from Saturday visits to asking your child to stay at your place for a few days, if you cut your partner out of the scene completely? Do not, therefore, commit yourself to a scheme forbidding this contact. You will be told that it "will be very distressing for the children." What this means is that the idea is very distressing to the former spouse. It cannot be nearly as distressing as, for example, heated arguments between parents, or losing contact with one parent. What it usually does is satisfy curiosity, more than anything else.

It could be different if you split up with your (new) partner and introduce somebody else who seems less appealing. A number of children have said to me with some regret that "Daddy never seems to be able to nail down the right one," or words to that effect. If you have a succession of friends, you must expect that your child will feel involved: some changes will be applauded, while others will be a cause for sadness.

Sometimes not meeting the "other" woman or the "other" man is turned into a bargaining point, to get more frequent access, or to pay less alimony, or whatever. Keep this right off the bargaining-table if you can. Apart from all else, your partner will not want to feel like a pawn on a chessboard. It also represents a concession to the politics of revenge, which inevitably lead to bitterness.

THE "NEW" DADDY (OR MOM)

Like the "other" woman this person may be of either sex. When your former spouse marries again, or forms a new partnership with someone living in, it will have an effect on your children and probably on your links with them.

Their attitude towards this person will vary from one extreme to the other. This makes predicting the effects very difficult. What you *may* find is one or more of the following.

Less time available

This may not happen at once, but the new step-parent will almost certainly want to share some activities with your child, and these will take up time. You may be competing for weekend afternoons. Some delicate compromises will be necessary.

Loyalty conflict

Your child may suddenly feel torn between liking the newcomer and wanting to remain on good terms with you. He may feel he ought to choose. Don't pressure him to do so. After all, why shouldn't he like and admire both of you, if you each have something to offer? The best solution is for your child to be able to see the two of you, occasionally, shaking hands and perhaps finding some common ground. If he feels he can talk naturally and openly to you both, it is much less of a burden for him.

Resentment of being supplanted

Especially in the situation where an elder or an only son finds his mother is getting married again, there can be very strong resentment of being edged out of the role of mainstay and source of comfort to the parent who has had custody. You may find, then, that an appeal is made to you to return or help fight off the intruder. You may even be asked if your child could now live with you, instead.

Resist the temptation to feel superior. It is great that your child can confide in you, and talk over the problem. But don't believe everything you hear about the undesirability of the newcomer. Bear in mind that the resentment may decay if your child is made to feel that he still has a key position in his home and in his other parent's affections. Keep an open door if your child wants to come and stay for a while, but regard this as a temporary visit. Do a lot of listening, and help out by suggesting ways of being tactful at home. Ask to meet the newcomer, if possible, and look for the good side as well as what you've been told. In the long term, your child may regard you as more generous and wise if you point out the good side in this person and act as a shrewd peacemaker rather than joining the rush to the barricades.

Problems with names

Your child may be asked to call the new person "Daddy" or "Mom," and this may go against the grain. Depending on the age of the child, step-parents nowadays are perhaps more inclined to suggest using a first name instead, but there are exceptions. Your inclination may be to enter the fight, to preserve the principle that only *you* are the "Daddy" in question. But it's best to steer clear. You don't have to live with the effects of a running battle all week long. If your child asks you if he can go on calling you "Daddy," or if he wants to change to your Christian name, why not go along with what seems to make him more comfortable? It is in fact flattering to be asked. Anything that strengthens the feeling that he can relax with you, talk freely, and get strength from being with you should be supported.

Conflicts: customs, behavior, accent, dress, etc.

The new step-parent may have ideas about how to behave that are different from yours. These ideas may be translated into rules that your child now has to obey. Well, if you do not have shared custody, there is virtually nothing you can do about this. Stick to your own rules, in your own home, and whenever you are with your child. But avoid stirring up a revolt—by suggesting, for example, that if your teenage child wants to smoke at home (in defiance of a new rule) he should take the package you're offering, and go ahead and light up. Nobody is going to gain from that. If your child appeals to you about new rules, advise him that it's best to raise the issue in the open, and ask to discuss it, rather than waging a silent war of resistance. Talk to him about the art of compromise, and remind him that when he goes off to live on his own he will be at perfect liberty to rewrite any rules he wants.

Step-parent stories

These are a dime a dozen. Don't believe everything you hear, especially from impressionable seven- and eight-year-olds, who readily imagine themselves in fairy stories and end up believing that it is all happening. Other children are often contributors to this:

when they hear that a friend of theirs is going to have a step-mother, they say, "Don't take any apples from her, whatever you do." If you see *evidence* of mistreatment, or sense that your child is not so much excited by having a story to tell as hating it, then that is another matter. You must raise the problem immediately with those who are responsible for it. If you feel uneasy after such a meeting, go straight to the local Children's Aid, and talk the matter over there. It may well be better for a third party to keep a watch on what is going on.

NEW BROTHERS AND SISTERS

Your new partner may have children too. Perhaps they are going to live with you, perhaps not. But at some stage your child and these other children are going to meet. What will they make of each other? When they meet for the first time, there is no telling how this will work out. Where the numbers are even on both sides—one and one, or two and two, etc.—the chances of rapid success are considerably greater. Where it's a case of two and one, there are often immediate problems. It's too easy for the two to gang up on the one. This single child is forced to make the transition from being the center of things to being odd man out. Alternatively, it may work out that whichever of the pair of children is closer in age to the single child tries to recruit him in the battle he is currently fighting against his sister or brother.

If something like this happens, and there is fighting instead of play, remember that in schools it is happening all the time. They have to work out a way of getting along. This will be more success-ful, if:

1 : You don't command them to be friendly to each other.

2 : You realize that while some children *like* each other, others simply *tolerate* each other. (Therefore, don't expect too much by way of laughter and co-operation: play in parallel is not a bad form of coexistence.)

3 : You apply the same house rules to both.

4 : If necessary, you tell each to respect the other's personal property, and his own space in the house.

5 : You let at least one fight run its course (up to, that is, the moment where it gets dangerous). Children often need to work off aggression or to test each other. Their relations are often much better afterwards, unless one child is really disturbed, so that he is spoiling for a fight all the time. (At that point, your child needs psychological help.)

6 : You and your partner enforce similar rules, and share out favors equally between the two sides.

There is very little published research into this question, but my interviews suggest that it makes very little difference whether the children who are thrown together suddenly are of the same sex or not, or the same age or not. Interests in common, whether these are music, football or macrame, usually contribute to getting along well together, unless one is far more advanced than the other and gloats about it. Discourage gloating, if you suspect it, and encourage the idea of giving help.

Some of you will find that the parent with custody will not allow visits to the other house by your partner's children, even when invited by your child. Try to anticipate this, by sounding out reactions in advance, to avoid any children being embarrassed or hurt.

When you have new children by your partner, you provide your child with half-brothers or half-sisters. This is rather different. It gives your child the chance to be in on the scene from the start. Don't be coy about it. Tell him what is happening, so that he hears it first from you. Let him see some of the preparations, just as you would if you were telling him about a new full brother or sister.

This can be a very big experience for him, especially if there is no immediate prospect of the same thing at his other parent's home. He deserves to share in some of the excitement, so that he can learn from it, and develop a good relationship with the new addition.

He may be jealous at first. It would be amazing if he were not. But a child who gets advance warning, and later is allowed to help prepare a baby's bath, set out the oil, find the diaper pins, and the rest, will feel too important to be jealous for long.

He might also be anxious for his other parent, particularly if maintenance is being paid and he has been warned that there will be less money coming in if you have a new child. This kind of fear is fairly easy to detect. If he is old enough to feel responsible, you should explain what changes there may be, and why. Better to draw his fire, if need be, than to make him resentful of the baby. Sometimes children—mainly girls, but not exclusively—get so carried away by a baby's arrival that they can talk of little else. Advise them to keep this to school, and to talk about it at their home only if asked. Tact will help everybody.

THE EXTENDED FAMILY

One of the sad features of divorce is the way grandparents sometimes lose touch with their grandchildren. If the family has moved right across the country, there is not a great deal to be done. But you can still, for example, remember an elderly uncle who never sees the children nowadays, when you are ordering holiday photographs. Keeping these people in touch with your child's progress is one thing, but you should also remind your child from time to time who there is exactly on your side of the family. Otherwise, many years hence he may have only a vague idea of who his relations are. One Saturday parent I know was stunned when his fourteen-year-old son asked him, "Who are those two old people in the photo on the wall?" "But—they're your grandparents." Then he worked it out. One had died, the other was in a nursing-home. The last time his son had seen the old man was six years previously. He knew next to nothing about these people. But could he be blamed?

One good idea for a wet afternoon is to work out a family tree. Whatever happens, then, your child will know something about the various branches. Pay some visits together, too. You may find that, just as your own imagination is running down, one of your relatives comes up with some fascinating things to see or do.

Giving your child the feeling of belonging to a much larger group may be one of the best ways in which you can help him. Tell him what was special about the names in the family tree, whether they had happy lives or sad. Bring them alive for him.

Whether or not you have broken ties with your ex-spouse's family depends on them as well as on you. They may not like to see you with the children, out of a feeling of loyalty to the other side. But this rather old-fashioned attitude is breaking down gradually. If your children have an impulse to stop off at your brother-in-law's house while you are driving by, that is a natural instinct which does not deserve suppressing. You may be doubtful about it, but give it a try. He may be waiting for you to make the first move. Only adults feel that families should be split in this way. Children certainly don't: they are much more sensible about that sort of thing.

9 : Making a Fight of It

There is no point whatever in going to lawyers or to the courts if you can possibly avoid it. This bald statement ignores the exceptions: for some, a lawyer is the only sympathetic person they can trust. I do not deny the value of this. But, if you can, solve your own problems.

At times, such as when a divorce is arranged, you cannot do without the law. For reasons of convenience as well as money, some marriages simply split up and the ex-spouses take up with new partners without the formalities of becoming unmarried and remarried. This is not the book in which to argue the rights and wrongs of this. But it is relevant to point out that avoiding legal formality can lead to untidy problems where maintenance obligations are concerned, and also the questions of custody of the children, influence on their schooling and how to continue relationships with both of the parents. This makes it seem sensible to arrange for at least one brief visit to a courtroom, so that everyone understands the basic rules.

This visit, in fact, need only be made by the lawyers. Custody and access arrangements, as indeed most divorce detail, can be handled at arm's length. All that is needed are letters of consent from both parents, in wording agreed between the lawyers. (This assumes, of course, that both parties agree.)

Protracted legal games are or should be exclusively a pursuit of the rich. The pressure should be considerable before you reach for the button marked "lawyer."

First, consider the realities of the system. The following holds good for most parts of the United States and Canada, but the laws and practice vary from state to state—for example there is a trend towards awarding joint custody in California. Once the terms of custody and access are fixed by court order, there are very few instances where either parent can succeed in getting them changed, if the parents are in dispute. Court officials like to see things fixed once and for all, partly because they do not wish to confuse children any further, and partly because they tend to support the *status quo* until it is very obvious that change is required. If you and your former spouse can *agree* on a new format, change comes more easily.

If you feel you must talk to a lawyer about something to do with custody or access, don't go without a very clear idea in your mind of what exactly you want to achieve. Remind yourself that his time costs money. Before you give him a call, if you have a low income, check out first whether you might be entitled to free legal advice. If you just want a preliminary check on whether you have a justifiable cause for complaint or a reasonable chance of getting it put right through the law, it makes sense to try there first. You may of course feel that you are entitled to legal aid, and that this will cover all your costs. Unfortunately it doesn't always work out like that. It may be decided, after an application has been made—and after you have already started to get involved—that you are entitled only to a proportion of your outlay. This cannot always be predicted, although a better lawyer will be able to assess your chances more accurately.

A lawyer is not a shark. Not if he is a typical lawyer, that is. But he is human. He has to make a living like anybody else, and he has to charge realistically for his time. It doesn't matter whether this time is spent talking to you, writing to another lawyer, or simply thinking about the problem you have raised with him. Everything costs.

Sometimes one ex-spouse recognizes this point while the other does not. This leads to everything becoming organized through a lawyer, including arrangements for access and even picking up the children. In the end, if maintenance is being paid, the amount that is eventually used for the welfare of either of the two ex-spouses, and most certainly of the children, diminishes proportionately. This can prove a harsh lesson.

Approximately one in every four of the many separated and divorced parents I have spoken to has admitted during the interview that he (or she) regrets and resents not realizing at the time that the legal taximeter was remorselessly ticking away.

There is another important argument against having recourse to the law after the divorce is finalized. What it does is to extend the period of the divorce activity. Divorce, in terms of a splitting that causes pain, is something to be got out of the way quickly to make way for *post-divorce*. You know perfectly well what each envelope embossed with the name of the legal firm means to you. It is a warning shot, if not an actual missile. Hostilities, it declares, are still open. You have almost certainly received more than one, and you know how nervously or angrily you react to them, whether they are sent on by your own firm or not. Try to solve whatever it is in a different way if you can, so that the atmosphere in which a solution gets worked out is better for you, for your ex-partner, and for your children. Your bank balance will benefit too.

Despite all this, there comes a time when you feel you *have* to take a battle into the lawyers' offices, and perhaps into the courts. The commonest situations for this (excluding falling behind in maintenance, if that applies) are these: not getting the access that was agreed and stipulated in the court order; anxiety that your child is being harmed, physically or mentally, and that joint custody or transfer of custody should be arranged. These may, of course, all be compounded into one intricate problem, but they are better visualized separately.

Assume you are not getting the access to which you are entitled. For some time you have been trying to arrange a visit to see your child of five. In theory you should have obtained this every two weeks as a minimum. But three months have gone by during which you have encountered stone-walling on the telephone, refusal to answer letters, a locked door and no answer to the bell when you arrive at an appointed time. You have been told through a relative or a friend in common that your ex-spouse would prefer you not to see your child again, that you are believed to be a bad influence on him, and that the child doesn't want to see you anyway.

This adds up to a sticky situation. And it happens all the time. Don't think that your case is the first.

You must understand that the law can probably help you here a little way, but only so far. The rest is really up to you, and to your skills at diplomacy.

In the situation described above you have ample reason to suppose you are being deliberately edged out of your child's life. You don't want that, and you will make a fight of it. Very well. First write to your ex-spouse in these terms, firmly but without hysteria: you consider that your right to access is being unreasonably obstructed, and that you feel this is wrong for your child as well as for yourself. Plead for a simple arrangement to see your child every second Sunday for a month or so—as a trial period, if that is preferred. Then add with regret that, if you cannot see eye to eye on this, you will have to take your case to a lawyer. Keep a copy of this letter, and of any reply that you get.

This may work—well, fine! You've saved a lot of time and trouble. Now make a success of it.

But if it *doesn't* work explain briefly to your lawyer what your problem is and what steps you have taken. Now give him a piece of paper (prepared and waiting in your pocket) that shows clearly all the important facts, with dates. Don't make it a life history—two pages at the most. He will want to see the court order and any other legal documents you may have, too. Include references to any appointments you made for visiting your child that were broken. This will save valuable time. Ask your lawyer to write a brief letter to your former spouse, on the lines of your last warning, but leaving the door still open for a trial period of visits.

This often works. It shows, after all, that you mean business. But it depends on your being prepared to argue and compromise a little on the precise visiting arrangements that are to be made when an answer arrives and you make contact again. Never expect a total victory. The best way back towards a pleasant atmosphere for your child when you visit him is for both sides to feel that they have won something.

As soon as you feel that access is again negotiable, try to get a relative or friend involved too—perhaps to meet the child on the first couple of visits. (Note that your ex-spouse may feel differently about letting down somebody else from letting you down.) Call your lawyer and thank him politely for doing his job. Don't suggest he keeps a close eye over all subsequent proceedings. But keep records of what happens, and of any messages or letters, in case you need to take them back to him later.

Let's assume again that you fail once more. All demands, including your lawyer's letter, are ignored. Now choose exact dates and times that you want for a few visits, starting a month away. Make sure they are consistent with the court order. Tell your lawyer you want to press this schedule. His next letter will put these requests clearly, adding that his client is prepared to vary one or two of the times should they prove to be particularly difficult. If so, could he be phoned immediately? He draws attention to the fact that the schedule is entirely consistent with the court order. The question is then put: "Could an answer please be given in ten days confirming acceptance of the proposal?" Otherwise, the letter continues, with regret the case will be brought before the court at the earliest opportunity. In this case, could the name and address of the lawyer who would act for the other side please be forwarded?

If this works, and it sometimes does, either before or after the point where the parent with custody actually consults a lawyer, you will have achieved something positive with a little expense, but not *that* much. Note that you have not demanded redress, accused the other party of heartlessness, or spiced your letters with invective and with witty barbs. All that simply stiffens resistance, takes longer, and costs more. Further, you have kept your demands clear and simple. Making them complicated offers too many grounds for argument. There has to be an element of threat in the last letter, particularly. But this has to be put in such a way as to show you would hate to go as far as the court. A naked threat should always be avoided. Even if someone gives way to it, they *remember* it. Sooner or later they find a way to pay you back, possibly even through your child. Nor do you want anything in either your or your lawyer's letters that could be used as evidence of harassment.

The last letter needs to go by registered mail, with recorded delivery.

From this point on, if you are still not successful, several things may happen. If you think about the possibilities in advance, you can work out what action you should take in advance. There are five main possibilities.

The first is that your former spouse (directly or through a lawyer) tells you that certain conditions must be met before access to the children will be provided. These conditions usually subdivide into requests for more money; requests for fewer, more controlled visits (for example in certain places, in front of certain people, etc.) or for certain places or certain people to be avoided during visits.

The second possibility is that a series of reasons is given (with or without the threat of these being paraded in court) explaining why you should not visit your son, or why you should retire permanently from his life. These reasons will probably be a mixture of logic and emotion.

Third, there may be a sudden move to a different district, town or country. (The likelihood of this tactic, which is not uncommon, increases if you are paying little or no maintenance.)

Fourth, one of a number of delaying moves is made, for example the announcement of illness via a relative, etc.

The fifth possibility is that your challenge may be picked up, and a legal struggle cannot be avoided.

Note that the first, second and fourth examples above are in fact opportunities for negotiation, as much as problems. Here is where a lawyer can often see a way through, while you are perhaps too emotionally involved to spot the easiest way out of the maze. He has his experience of what is a real demand, and what is merely a bargaining point. He can discuss with his opposite number how that case might sensibly and quickly be resolved. You must, however, make it clear to him *what you want* as a minimum, and what you are prepared to trade off. Otherwise he cannot operate to your best advantage.

The third example presents an added dimension of difficulty. Anyone with custody of the child may take him to another town, *but* the other parent can usually, at least in theory, exercise a right to keep the child in the same country. The difficulty is to know what to do *before* it happens. It is rare for anyone to be extradited from a country with a child if he or she has custody of that child. The main reason for extradition would be overstaying the terms of a visa, or making a false declaration in order to get an entry permit. You can get your lawyer to enforce your rights of access within the country itself, after removal. But, even where there is a history of reciprocal legal agreements between countries, two court actions may be required—one in each country—before your right to a holiday with your child would be granted—assuming the fight is drawn out all the way. In 1978 a British father obtained a court order in his own country allowing him two weeks' holiday with his young children, to be taken within a certain time period. This was appealed against successfully by the mother before a court in Nebraska, where she had taken the children.

The situation in the fifth example, where battle is joined, needs to be understood if it is going to be dealt with properly. There are several reasons why a battle may be wanted: eager anticipation of an aggressive set-to in court, with maximum publicity, since there is a certain amount of ammunition against you (relevant or irrelevant) which is going to be used; belief that your case can be overturned in court; desire to re-open the whole divorce settlement and seek new terms for a court order.

Try to work out in your mind what the intentions are on the other side. If your former spouse wants publicity, to pursue the war against you in the open, you must decide whether you can actually stomach this, and (more importantly) how your children are going to be affected by a fierce court action. If the intention, however, is to adjust the terms of the court order, the lawyers can reach some kind of compromise on what to do if they are instructed as to what would be acceptable. It is rare for both sides to be really convinced that they are going to win, *unless* they have not been listening to their solicitors, and getting a more realistic idea of what is and what is not likely. Thus there are ways of avoiding the final commitment to a court-room drama, right up to the end. It is always worth exploring them.

But let's assume that you end up in court. Your case is presented, and it is a solid one. But here comes the catch. The court is told that your child has no wish to see you. This may be something you don't believe. But, in terms of what is actually going to happen after the court is cleared, the reactions of your child are rather important.

I deliberately chose the age of five for this example. Up to this age, most courts will assume that whatever a child may be said to feel about the Saturday parent there is no reason why they should not be put together every now and then to see how they get on. An adolescent, by contrast, will speak his own mind, and that is that. Between five and twelve is the difficult area. In a family court, a judge may retire and ask to talk to the child privately, to gauge how strong his feelings are, and whether this should affect the issue. He can call for reports from a welfare worker or a court psychologist. On occasion, this can develop into a battle between expert witnesses, but people who are experienced in family disputes usually recognize the difference between a temporary mood, a set conviction, and a put-up job. At five, it will *probably* be assumed that your child's expressed (or reported) wish not to see you will be overruled. But from this point on the likelihood of the child influencing the outcome increases progressively, and you must be prepared for this.

Another catch. You have won your case, but will you actually see your child? There are plenty of cases of Saturday parents winning in court but only rarely, if ever, seeing their children again. If the parent with custody is *determined* you should not see your children, that parent will win nine times out of ten. Unfair, perhaps, but true.

You turn up at an appointed time, as directed by the court. Your child is in bed, and you are told he is sick. Or a journey may have been made to a distant city the previous day, and the last train was missed. Any number of excuses may be offered, which may be very hard to contradict.

Note that having a court order does *not* empower you to barge inside and demand to see for yourself whether your child is really ill or not. You have no right of entry into the other home. (In fact, somebody may even be waiting to photograph you breaking the law.)

So what happens? You could go back to your lawyer, and ask him to see that the order gets enforced. You will get some sympathy but no magic wand. No one is going to fine the former spouse, or commit her to prison for contempt. Reversing a custody order is possible here, but lengthy and on the whole unlikely. The more plausible the excuses for not complying with the order for access are made to seem, the stronger the forces against you become. No court is going to risk letting the children suffer if there is a chance that the excuses given may be valid.

Some pressures may be applied on your behalf. These depend rather on local custom and the disposition of the people concerned. A welfare officer (more rarely, a policeman) is sent along to try to arrange another appointment for a visit. He may also come round with you, to discourage reneging.

But neither of these people is really going to change an embattled mind.

The sooner you can get back into personal negotiation, the better. The law may help you to win a breakthrough, but for the future you have to help yourself. The law is a very expensive crutch. Apart from that, officials tend to lose patience with people who do not show signs of being able to deal with their own problems in the end. If you win a visit, make it work; and look for the right moment to be conciliatory.

If you win such a visit, it's best not to talk about the legal proceedings, unless your child wants to talk about them himself. In no circumstances should you blame him for any part he may have played in it. You want to get back on good terms, quickly. Involve a relative or a friend if you can. Someone who has an objective viewpoint, and credibility, may become useful in the future if they observe you with your child. Get them to take photographs if possible. Widen the circle of those who can say ''Of course they had a good time that day,'' although you will naturally want some time alone too, just the two of you.

You may be very surprised, later on, when you are informed that ''He burst into tears as soon as he got back, had terrible nightmares, and wet his bed when told you were going to take him away again.'' In fact, some dramatic changes are to be expected when the child loves both parents and doesn't know what to make of the battles that have raged around him. You had a good time, but there may be some truth in this. How much is exaggerated, you don't know. What is certain is that the sooner the atmosphere is defused the better for all of you. And meanwhile you will need some evidence that you are reliable, friendly, and good for your child to be with for a few days.

The assumption here is that you *do* get on well with your child. It might not be quite so rosy if he is older, and if there has been a considerable gap during which he has only been exposed to one side of the story. Occasionally there are cases where a child has become terrified of an absent parent as a result of a long and effective propaganda campaign. This makes it hard. You want two things which may seem incompatible. You want your children to get to know you properly, but you don't want them to suffer genuine anxiety at the prospect of meeting you and staying with you. In this situation, the longer you put it off, the more difficult it is going to be to achieve any change of attitude. Make an early start if you can. But do not try to do too much too quickly. One confrontation does not overcome prejudice.

Gradually increase the information your child has about you in a lot of different ways. Short, frequent meetings, in different circumstances, will start to restore trust. Do no overreact when your child comes out with something like: "We're very poor, because you took away all Mommy's money." Don't shout about the alimony you pay, or the house you left behind. Instead, say pleasantly, "No, that's not so"—assuming it isn't so—and show by action rather than words that you are a generous person, and a thoughtful person who worries about money too, sometimes. Don't load the child up with gifts, because this only makes you seem a soft touch, and a guilty one at that. Show it by making sure he is comfortable, eats a square meal, and gets time to play with you and talk to you. If he seems to need a new pair of jeans or running shoes, see if you can't shop for some. Ask after your former spouse. Stop off somewhere before the visit ends, and ask him if he'd like to buy something to take back to that person.

The aftermath of a legal tangle takes time to settle down in a child's mind, and in his relationship with an absent parent. But, provided he gets the idea that *you* are hanging up your six-guns, he will ease back into a more comfortable way of looking at his parents.

There is also the situation, referred to at the beginning of this chapter, of a resolute determination to wipe one parent out of a child's life while at the same time giving that child a hard time. There is a fine line here between stern discipline and abuse. When the line is crossed, the absent parent feels desperate. The law has a very difficult problem in deciding for the best. On the one hand there is sympathy for an unhappy child, but on the other is the conviction that, if both parents are in dispute over changes to a court order, that order is best left unchanged.

One child of eight, FJ, was kept for nearly three months in a shed, apparently for disobedience. His mother and step-father claimed they had to put him in there for punishment because he stole, swore, fought, kicked, threatened the baby, and was otherwise hard to control. His father, who had only succeeded in seeing FJ by waiting in side-streets for him to appear, was convinced that the punishment was in fact for going out with *him,* and for refusing to call his stepfather "Daddy." When discovered by police (who were called in after a social worker had followed up an anonymous phone call), FJ was not in a fit condition to add to the arguments, one way or the other. He needed a few days in hospital for exposure, weakness probably caused by undernourishment, and sores. Both parents now wanted him back.

The treatment FJ had received, while meriting a stern caution, was not felt to warrant any kind of prosecution. A social worker talked to the mother and the stepfather, and reported that there was a good chance that the family would get on better from then on, based on a better understanding of each other's needs. The police and those in the State Children and Youth Service Department avoid, as a rule, bringing this kind of thing into court if it doesn't seem likely to do more good than harm. This particular case was perhaps a marginal one. But FJ's father was advised by his lawyer, who made some inquiries, that he stood little chance of getting custody. FJ was talked to, but was not actually consulted. (The age of eight comes into that gray area where some authorities will give weight to the opinions of the child but others will not.)

If everyone's personality had been slightly different, it is possible that the authorities' decision would have been absolutely right. In retrospect, it was clear that FJ hated his stepfather, who was very jealous of FJ's father. FJ and his mother had unpredictable ups and downs. Her young baby claimed a lot of her energy and attention.

FJ's father was in a stronger position to get visits, now, because the stepfather felt obliged to fit in with the rules. There were two meetings. During the second outing together, his father felt that FJ could do with a plaid jacket that had a warm lining. The boy wore it that afternoon, and returned home with it on.

The exact sequence from then on is uncertain. The stepfather lost his temper, and thrashed FJ. The coat probably served as a trigger, although there may have been other factors. The jacket was thrown out, where it was noticed by neighbors among the garbage. Not much is known about the following three weeks, during which the father was told that FJ had a bad cold (twice), and refused to see him (once).

Then FJ was in hospital again. This time he had drunk some liquid weedkiller that had been diluted ready for use and stored in an unmarked container under the kitchen sink. His precise motivation in tasting it, and then going on to drink it, is again a matter for conjecture. Possibly he only wanted to get his mother's attention again. But at least one social worker believes he was looking for a way out of an impossible situation. He is in a chronic care ward, his organs permanently damaged. He gets visits from both his parents now, so in a sense he did win something.

Was his father actually to blame for what happened? His father is still kicking himself. "I just didn't go at it hard enough," he complains. Interestingly, he does not blame the authorities, although one local newspaper hauled them over the coals. But it is not easy to determine exactly what his father might have done to help FJ. Going further with his lawyer, and through the courts, would have cost more than he possessed. Legal aid might have helped him a little, but not enough.

A richer man, with better contacts, could have done one or more of the following:

First, he could have asked for a second, or a third legal opinion.

Second, he could have arranged for his lawyer to get a specialist's opinions on the basic issues in the case, and the prospects for reversing the custody award, together with an indication of the best means—in terms of what would be relevant ground.

Third, he could have arranged to discuss everything with officials at the local Children's Aid offices.

Fourth, he could have discussed the potential dangers in the situation with his minister, his elected representative, the family doctor, the social worker, the school—in short, with *any* interested party who might have proved helpful. One or more of these might have been directly influential, or might have observed, taken notes, intervened when necessary.

Note that a richer person has the benefit of *time* to do all this, as well as being unconcerned about travelling expenses. What it adds up to should come as no surprise: there is a law for the rich, and a law for the poor.

Even a really wealthy man might have failed to help and get custody of FJ. But the odds would have been much more fair.

Notice that the third and fourth examples above are things which FJ's father could have pursued without spending so much. Admittedly, he would have needed time off work. But buttonholing people with some power at their disposal is an art as well as being free for anybody to try. It needs a mixture of firmness and diplomacy, knowing when to jam one's foot in the door and when to disarm with a smile. Avoid hangdog looks and hysterical outbursts: these only serve to convince an official that you *are* the wrong person to have custody. But be as firm and pertinacious as you dare. The stronger, more persistent voices get listeners. If you are in serious doubt about the safety of your child, but the authorities are not helpful:

Demand to see and talk to a superior.

Find out the *home* telephone numbers of the officials who are proving hard to get, and discuss your problem more fully with them *in the evenings*.

Talk to some local newspaper reporters to see if they have any helpful contacts; they may show an interest themselves.

You may be amazed how well these tactics sometimes work. Even if you don't get everything you want, some responsible people will be watching a case more carefully. This can't be bad.

The next case study is instructive in showing the borderline that the police often observe before deciding to step in.

Wanda shared a stormy marriage for fourteen years before it broke up. By then there were two children, Paul (twelve) and Debbie (ten). One day, after a particularly bitter scene, Wanda packed a small suitcase and went to her sister's for a few days. On her return, the locks were all changed, and the children were inside. From an upstairs window her husband told her to go away, and talk through lawyers.

She did so. For three years she has been struggling to see her children again. They have contrived three brief meetings throughout that time.

The husband played his hand callously but skillfully, until he made one mistake. Here are some examples of his tactics.

He persuaded her to let one lawyer (his own) handle the whole divorce sequence.

He persuaded the children that their mother had become a prostitute, and that naturally they should stay with him.

He arranged for a teacher at the children's school, who had passed messages from Wanda to her daughter, to be transferred.

He contrived by using a series of different excuses, each superficially valid, to prevent Wanda exercising any visiting rights, except for one weekend visit and two meetings after school.

He harassed her each time she attempted to contact the children or lodge complaints through her lawyer or through the police. (Some examples: her car lights would be kicked out in a car park; she would get phone calls at half-hour intervals through the night; threats would be made to anyone who visited her; etc.) It must be obvious that this was a man with wealth and influence as well as strength of purpose. This makes him much harder to fight. Wanda's first (own) lawyer advised her to leave the country and start afresh.

The police would have nothing to do with it, apart from murmuring sympathetically, until:

Wanda's husband remarried. This made any harassment, in their eyes, no longer a husband-and-wife affair, and they showed a keener interest. (Divorced pairs still count as pairs.)

He overreached himself by informing the police anonymously that Wanda's flat was used as a brothel, which led them to make an abortive raid one evening when she and a girl friend were giving a party.

Now more vigilant, the police called the ex-husband to congratulate him on giving them a useful tip-off. He fell obligingly into the trap, and became open to prosecution for "causing a public mischief." He is on probation. But he still has custody. The older the children get, the more they are regarded as mature, and able to choose for themselves. The less they see of their mother, the less they can judge what she might be like to live with.

Wanda continues to press for access. The issue is still in doubt. This is a reminder that the law positively dislikes getting involved in either marital or post-marital arguments. It also shows dramatically what can happen when somebody exploits possession of the children and is determined to influence them permanently. Once people are in separate households, on a permanent basis, and an actual offense is committed, then it is another question. In fact, the police may sometimes make up for lost time in such cases, where they suspect one party of arrogance. If you are in Wanda's situation, you may have to wait until your ex-spouse oversteps the mark: then you must take all the records of the event you possibly can, and encourage observers (if any) to become witnesses. It may be your one chance, and you have to seize it.

The children in the above case had to face an unpleasant choice twice over. Think of it briefly from the child's point of view. Choosing with which parent to live means *rejecting* the other one. They do not have to be very old to feel this. Many dislike it, and feel guilty afterwards. Some go around trying to justify the decision a long time later. In this kind of tug-of-love situation, even if you win, you can help the children a lot by making it clear to them that rejection need never be total. Encourage an open-door policy and, if they announce they want to visit your former spouse for a few days, help them to fix up what they need. If they suspect you of giving way to revenge, after you have got back what you wanted, they will respect you all the less.

Finally, lawyers like to win. They do not believe in pursuing a fifty-fifty case if they can avoid it, and get better odds for their clients. This is human, and professional. But sometimes they presume too far.

When Rachel and her husband split, their two daughters stayed with her. Andrew, fourteen, was asked if he, too, wanted to stay with his Mom. "No," he told her and his sisters, "You're all against him. I'm going to live with my dad. He needs somebody on his side."

Rachel's lawyer was aghast. "I can get a much better deal for you if you keep Andrew at home. Your maintenance package will be *much* higher, because the girls are already over sixteen. Tell him he's got to stay with you.''

She thought about this, and told Andrew, ''Take this door-key. Any time you want to come back to see me or your sisters, just turn up.''

''I valued his friendship *more*,'' she told me.

10 : Yes, It Matters

In the final analysis it is worth paying attention to what the children themselves are saying. While they are often critical of their Saturday parents for one reason or another, there are very few who criticize them for being there, or for keeping up the contact. They dislike being bored, being made to change too many of their own plans, or being tugged into the arena where the former married couple is still slugging it out. When any of those things happen, lack of enthusiasm for Saturday visits is hardly surprising. But they seem to sense when an effort has been made for their sake—that somebody keeps coming back, whether to go out and do things, or just to sit and talk. They take the point that this somebody actually cares about them sufficiently to want to do that. The indirect but clear message from this is that they themselves are worth something. A stronger self-image gives confidence and encourages people to set themselves higher goals in life.

Occasionally the sacrifices made by a Saturday parent are impressive to a child. But parading sacrifices of this kind is obviously wrong. Nobody appreciates being visited by a self-appointed martyr who does what he does simply to satisfy his own pride, rubbing his children's noses in his own presumed saintliness and sometimes making them feel throughly guilty. How a person looks at his difficulties is a personality factor that boils down to this question: Are you shouldering the burden for yourself or for your child?

In the case that follows the Saturday parent clearly put his children first. He profoundly influenced those children in a way that shows the principle of Saturday parenting passing through to a second generation.

According to his daughter Monica, Ben was unable to see his children in the regular way. He had no car because his welfare check would not stretch that far. Perhaps this was just as well, since he had an arthritic condition preventing his working with the skills he once possessed, and his driving might not have been very efficient. His ex-wife and two children lived far out in a suburb that was not well served by public transportation. There was no question of bringing the children over to *him*—in fact a large slice of Ben's disposable income had had to go into a legal firm for fighting to ensure that he got access at all.

Two helpful people in a church group took turns driving Ben out and back, and then out and back again (so he could return the children at the end of his Saturday visit.) This is an example of the way societies and groups of various kinds are beginning to see that in a modern situation there are new requirements to which they need to respond.

Even with this kindly help it demanded a lot of his energy to cross over town and try to be a normal father to two lively children who were ten and eight when the visiting began. Without much money, he couldn't take them to many shows. Joining in walks or sports was practically impossible, since prolonged or sudden movement was liable to be very painful. In reasonable weather they usually went to the park, where he picked a vantage point from which he could watch them play with friends they knew from going there often. Sometimes they went back to his apartment, and once or twice to a friend's home. A lot depended on how his legs and his back were feeling. Sometimes he had to phone and say he couldn't make it.

Once Monica herself was below par and joined Ben on a park bench, leaving her brother Joey to play touch football on the flat ground below. "He had a raincoat folded over his knees. Suddenly it slid to the ground. I was amazed when he tried to pick it up but couldn't. Right then he seemed far, far older than I'd ever imagined. I said to him, 'Daddy, you're *very* old.' He didn't have a quick come-back to that one. But he smiled and said, 'You pick it up then.' I remember that because I cringed later when I thought about the dumb thing I'd said. Joey and I treated him differently after that. Sometimes he told me to stop fussing him and acting like a nurse in hospital. But I realized something of what he was going through just to be with us. We didn't jump up on him and try to hang on his neck after that. And it made us think a bit more about people.

". . . Before he died when he was confined to his bed, Joey and I used to go over to the Seniors' Home and take him things."

Monica herself is divorced now, with a child aged five. She is glad that her ex-husband is positive about being a Saturday parent. She reckons that the relationship was good for her, in her time, and that there is no reason why it should not help her daughter too.

Without putting it into so many words, Monica and her brother were impressed by what their father was going through nearly every weekend, and by the fact that he was doing this from choice. She implied in the interview that if Ben expected anything in return he had not shown it. We can imagine that an arthritic man, unable to work, must have derived great satisfaction from achieving some good, happy meetings with his children despite his handicap. He may have noted with justifiable pleasure that his children were becoming considerate people too.

There are not all that many cases of Saturday parenting passing from one generation to the next in the same family. But it must be becoming more common. The trends in divorce rate promise precisely that. Among the many other valid reasons for visiting their absent children, future Saturday parents will think more and more to themselves, "I am setting an example to them. If and when they are in a similar situation, I would like to believe that they will care sufficiently to visit my grandchildren." At this moment such a point of view may still seem rather pessimistic. But there is so far no sign of any counter-trend that would stop this from being simply a realistic consideration.

If there is a danger in thinking too hard about Ben and Monica, it lies in encouraging a parent to expect too much. You cannot expect to receive visits yourself when you yourself come to need them. It simply cannot be supposed that your children will develop the same sense of priorities or of loyalties that you feel toward them yourself. Human history is a story of compromises between what is hoped for and what actually happens. What is certain are two things. If you see very little of them, you will mean very little to them. If you try to pressure them into feeling they have an obligation to see you when they are grown up, you are simply making the classic parental mistake of actually forcing them to run for cover. The net result is the same in both cases. Be thankful for compromises.

Every generation has the same problem. Parents conveniently forget their own resentment of pressure when they were young. They imply their children must be unnatural, ungrateful, not to want to spend weekends and Christmas with them. The same applies to both normal parents and to Saturday parents.

You will gradually see less and less of your children as they grow up—assuming that they are normal. Different interests, different ways of looking at life, curiosity about what it's like elsewhere, and—above all—the conflicting demands of friends, lovers, life-partners whether official or unofficial will all interpose themselves between you.

But you can recognize that there is the young adult whom you have helped grow into an independent person with a mind and spirit of his own. The *more* that he or she shows the ability to cope with life and make personal choices as an individual, the better the help you have given.

In any event by keeping up contact you have increased the chances that you will develop a lasting friendship between adults, based on mutual respect, not on obligations.

Sometimes a person who might have been a Saturday parent is sought out and the friendship starts without preliminaries. A woman who had introduced me to a Saturday parent for an interview told me later she had a special reason for wanting to help my book along. In her early twenties she suddenly felt an urge to find her father, who had left home while she was still an infant. From that day there had been no contact between them whatever. She described her urge as something she could not explain but which seemed to "sweep over" her, forcing her to go through every conceivable source to locate him. She called the scene when she finally saw him as one of the greatest days of her life. "I cried a lot because he was so nice—and it would have been so wonderful to have seen more of him, to have had him around when I was a kid." He told her he felt the same way.

What a waste of time! There can be no more eloquent way of stressing that Saturday parenting *does* matter—that you owe it to yourself and to your child to keep up contact.

Another social trend needs to be mentioned at this point. It is developing almost as fast as split families. In Canada in 1979, one in ten of all live births were to unmarried teenage girls. In the United States the figure is similar overall, although it varies greatly by area: from one in fifteen to one in five. Usually an unwanted teenage pregnancy comes as a great shock to parents, and it may seem impertinent to suggest that this could never happen to a child of yours. But it could. Consider this briefly: a pregnant teenager whose parents have split up has, logically, one more refuge open to her than another girl in the same predicament. She may get the sympathy and help she needs in the home of the parent with whom she is living. If so, that's fine. But if she doesn't, and if you have remained a friendly, known, and reliable person to her, then you could be her obvious port of call. It will be up to you to help.

This is by no means the only "trouble" in which a teenager may find himself or herself nowadays. It need not be as dramatic as a problem with drugs, drink, the police, or a social disease. It could be illness in the familial home, trouble with a step-parent, or simply an economic difficulty such as sudden loss of a job. The kinds of trouble that can impel a teenager to leave home are many and varied.

But teenage pregnancy stands out as a prime example in terms of sheer statistical likelihood. Surprisingly it only came up once in all the case histories studied. But in that one instance, the Saturday parent was able to provide shelter, and space in which his daughter was able to collect her thoughts and make plans without an emotional storm raging around her.

If you have kept an open door, various problems both major and minor may be brought to it. Often you may only have to be a sounding-board—an older adult who listens, occasionally offers advice, but more often just discusses. You will need to judge for yourself how far to be sympathetic, and when to explain why you consider something to be bad or wrong. But if you are accessible, and if you have made it obvious that you can be visited, at least the talking can begin.

Society as a whole is impatient with older teenagers. They are less obedient than they were as children, so that they cannot be organized to suit adults' convenience. Nor are they old enough to be expected to settle down and follow adult goals—that is, the goals that are recognized by *older* adults. Teenagers' difficulties seem less manageable. Both their tastes and their needs seem more expensive than society can remember at the same age. Memory is so short. This is part of the breakdown between young and old. As a Saturday parent you have given yourself a flying start in helping to redress the balance. You are not (in all likelihood) the parent most associated with day-to-day discipline and restrictions. You've probably had your differences. But you are mainly associated with a change of pace, and with the offering of an alternative view. You have become an obvious staging-post, to be visited during the difficult period in which the older teenager seems to have no contact with a society which is coldly rejecting him or her. Your eventual task, after the chilly walks across the park, from touch football to the milkshakes at Howard Johnsons on Saturday afternoons, could be a very big one. It could be up to you to close the generation gap.

So yes—both personally, and for society—you can bet it matters.

Bibliography

Blaine, Dr. G. B., Jr. "The Children of Divorce." *The Atlantic-Monthly,* March, 1963.

Bowlby, J. *Child Care and the Growth of Love*. Harmondsworth, England: Penguin Books, 1965.

Hennig, M. See in *Father's Influence on Children*. M. L. Hamilton. Chicago: Nelson-Hall, 1978.

Kelly, J. B. and J. S. Wallenstein. "The Effects of Parental Divorce-Experiences of the Child in Early Latency." *American Journal of Orthopsychiatry* 46(1) January, 1976. Published as *Surviving the Breakup*. New York: Basic Books, 1980.

Rosenthal, K. and H. Kesset. See in *Father's Influence on Children*. M. L. Hamilton. Chicago: Nelson-Hall, 1978.